# CAL

## Tribute
## to an
## American
## Hero

# TRIUMPH
### BOOKS

## York Daily Record

*York Daily Record* photo credits

Christopher Glass: pages 2–3, 4–5, 6, 9, 11, 17, 18–19, 20, 21, 48, 52, 55, 62, 69, 81, 82, 85, 86, 87, 92, 95 (bottom)

Brad Phalin: pages 25, 57, 91

Nicole Cappello: pages 26–27

Cisco Adler: pages i, 32–33, 34, 38, 50, 51, 54, 75 (bottom left), 78, 96

Paul Kuehnel: page 61

Phil Masturzo: page 75 (upper right)

# Foreword

When I first met him, Cal Ripken Jr. was tall and fair-skinned. He was a pretty good-looking kid.

His ice blue eyes were like that of an island lagoon. He had all of the tools of a great athlete.

But, on top of it all, what stuck out the most was his competitive desire. No matter what he wanted to do, he had to be the best.

From the very beginning, you just knew after watching him for awhile that he was something special. When he was just a kid taking batting practice off his father, he'd hit line drive after line drive at Memorial Stadium. That wasn't easy, even for veterans who already wore a major league uniform.

He had great hands and, for a big man, he moved smoothly through the infield. A combination of quiet confidence, poise, power, patience, and a lot of potential were part of his whole package.

He had a youthful exuberance that permeated the Orioles from his very first day with us.

There were some questions at first about how he might fit in, but Earl Weaver answered them all very quickly when he made Ripken the shortstop and batted him third—right in front of future Hall of Famer Eddie Murray.

Well, Earl was right. And after a bit of a slow start, Cal came around and

lived up to his billing. And a whole lot more.

By the standards back then, he was way too big to play short. But it didn't take long for him to change everyone's ideas and show what the new standard was going to be.

He has natural strength and, if you've ever been caught in one of his playful

headlocks, you'd know what I mean. Unfortunately, I had to be subjected to those headlocks every day for the three years we roomed together.

He had poise beyond his years and never seemed to feel the pressure like the rest of us.

He had the ability to stay in the moment and had an affinity for coming through in the clutch.

There just wasn't much he couldn't do out there. And from the very start he seemed like a seasoned veteran.

His quiet confidence led us to a World Series championship in 1983 and earned him the American League's Most Valuable Player award.

He was the best all-around player in the game and you'd never have known it.

He wasn't outspoken. He wasn't flashy. And he never seemed to have the controversial issues that follow most major league superstars.

He loved to have fun on the field. He loved to win.

And, come to think of it, Cal is still the best assistant prankster I've ever had.

—Rick Dempsey
August 16, 2001

Tribute to an American Hero

# Introduction: Images of Ripken Will Stay with Us Forever

Think about Cal Ripken Jr.

Close your eyes and visualize him.

Have an image?

OK, open your eyes and erase that one. Close your eyes again.

This time come up with another picture of Ripken.

If you like the Baltimore Orioles, if you're a baseball fan, or if you're just someone who pays attention to pop culture, surely you can do this exercise countless times and continue coming up with different snapshots.

Ripken reached the majors in 1981. He retired 20 years later at the end of the 2001 season after playing in nearly 3,000 games. It seems like he's always been in the spotlight.

He played in a sport with more games per season than any other at a time when cable TV and 24-hour sports channels were emerging. His sporting exploits have been filmed and photographed as much as or more than any other athlete in American history.

Subsequently, most of his greatest moments—captured by the media and frozen by time—linger in our minds well after the on-field heroics have ended.

So take the challenge and picture Cal Ripken.

What's the image you chose?

Is it the obvious one?

The balding, graying Ripken, in the picture's forefront, with one hand held high above his head while the background shows the illuminated numbers "2131."

That day—September 6, 1995, when Ripken officially broke Hall of Famer Lou Gehrig's consecutive-games streak of 2,130—was surely the most memorable Ripken moment for baseball lovers.

For many, it was the first game they had watched since baseball's 1994 labor strike. Ripken and his blue-collar work ethic brought them back, at least for an evening.

There are so many glorious images from that night to choose from. Like when his teammates pushed him out onto the field so he could properly thank the fans. Or when he spontaneously lapped the edges of the stands, grabbing the hands of adoring fans.

Or maybe it was when he embraced his wife Kelly and his two children.

Ripken is covered in champagne as the team celebrates in the locker room after they beat the Phillies in five games to win the 1983 World Series in Philadelphia on October 16. *Bettmann/Corbis archive*

Maybe you're just a baseball fan and what sticks with you is what happens between the lines. Maybe your lasting moment from that night is Ripken crushing a Shawn Boskie pitch over the outfield wall, putting a capper on the festivities.

After all, it's your visual slide show; you can choose what you want.

And maybe the Ripken of 1995 isn't the one you'll most remember.

Maybe your initial picture is the first time you ever saw the face and heard the name.

Was it that clip of Ripken in 1981 wearing a Rochester Red Wings cap and talking about

how he hoped to play for his hometown Orioles one day?

Or maybe you see him in 1982, with the brown locks flowing out of the three-colored hat with the cartoon oriole on the front. Back then, you probably thought to yourself, "What is a 6'4", 200-plus-pound guy doing at shortstop?"

Surely your mind can flicker from that image to Ripken accepting the American League Rookie of the Year Award in 1982 or the American League Most Valuable Player Award the following year.

He says his proudest moment came on October 16, 1983, at Veterans Stadium in

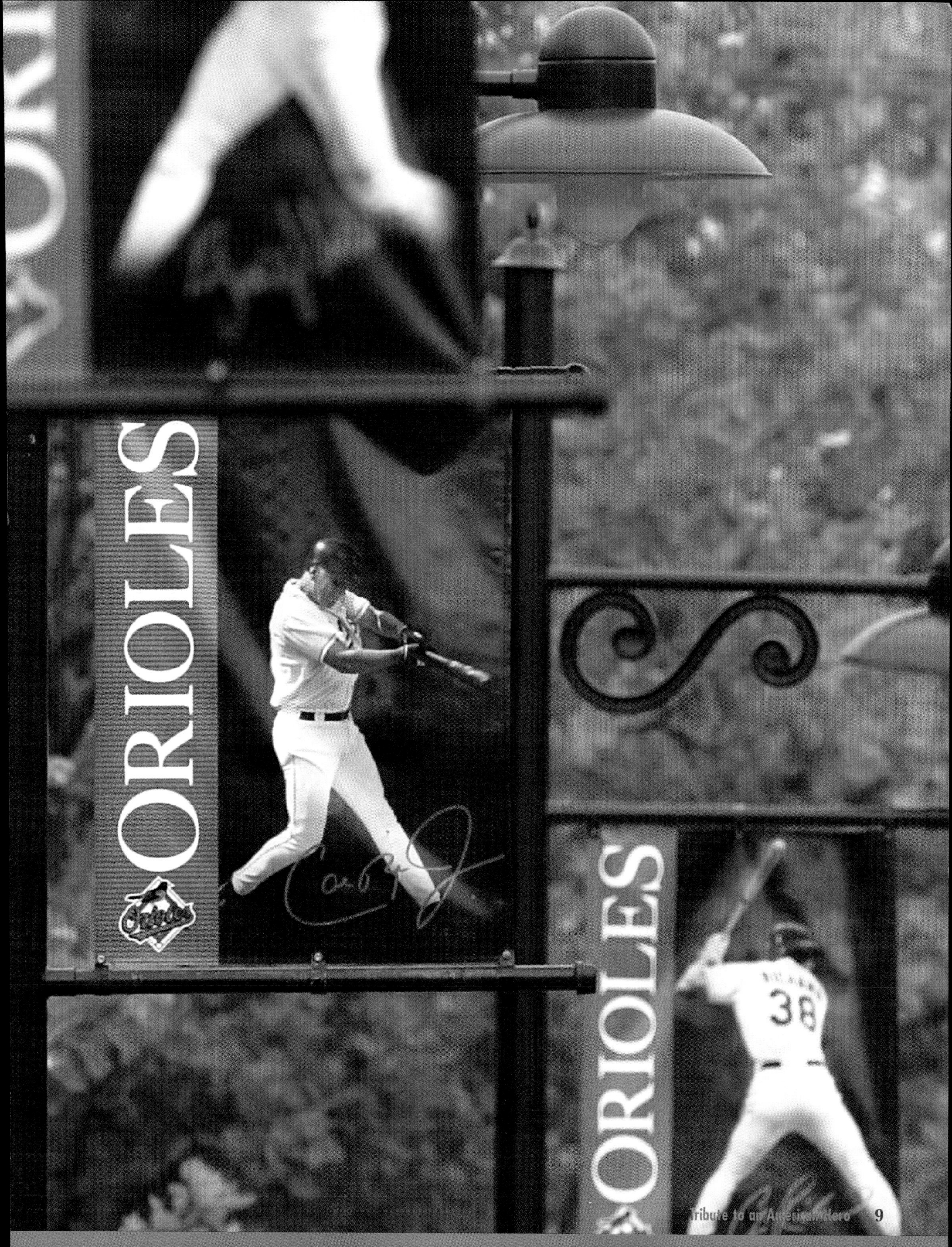
ORIOLES
ORIOLES
38

from his knees—moments that demonstrate how he won two Gold Gloves and set or tied 11 fielding records.

Throw in a home run or two from the 1991 season, when he hit a career-high 34 on his way to becoming only the 22nd player in history to win multiple MVP awards.

Make sure you have that snapshot of Ripken, his younger brother Billy, and their dad, Cal Sr., posing together on the front steps of Memorial Stadium's home dugout in 1987, when Cal Sr. became the first person in baseball's regular-season history to manage two sons on one team.

Don't forget the smiling Ripken with the white mustache above his top lip, part of the now-famous milk marketing campaign.

Or perhaps you remember a more pensive Ripken, like the one in late March 1999 who candidly discussed the death of his dad. Or the relieved Ripken, piercing blue eyes and a slight smile on his lips, announcing the end of The Streak on September 20, 1998.

Certainly, the most recent memories are the freshest. And when it comes to Ripken, those are worth remembering, too. Because what a year 2001 was for him.

After struggling at the plate in the two months prior to announcing his retirement,

Philadelphia. The Phillies' Garry Maddox hit a liner that Ripken caught in the bottom of the ninth inning to give the Orioles a World Series title—the only one of his career.

He carefully clutched that ball like a newborn child before darting toward the pitcher's mound. Yes, that one's probably in your mind's Cal Ripken photo album.

You must have room in there for a couple great defensive plays too—Ripken diving for a snow-cone catch or throwing out a runner the more relaxed Ripken returned to his old form in the summer months.

Close your eyes again and picture the 2001 All-Star Game.

Remember the standing ovation from the crowd at Safeco Field in Seattle?

Remember the flashbulbs popping as he approached the plate? Remember when he did the unthinkable, the remarkable— when he hit a home run during his 19th and final All-Star Game against Chan Ho Park?

You can probably still see him holding that game's MVP trophy and thanking the fans for being so supportive.

And let's not leave out the fans in our Ripken memories. Like the ones in Atlanta who gave him two curtain calls—one each for his two homers in his Turner Field finale.

Everywhere he went in his last season, fans showered him with gifts and applause. He responded with home runs in nearly every visiting stadium. And by signing autograph after autograph late into the night at each park.

His farewell tour was one of the most gripping in baseball history, from the announcement of the retirement to his last game in Baltimore to his final game in Yankee Stadium, the place Gehrig made his famous farewell speech decades before.

Now we must picture baseball without Cal Ripken, No. 8, the Iron Man.

Thankfully, though, Ripken left us with so many memorable moments in his sterling baseball career.

Moments we can experience again and again by simply closing our eyes. ■

*I*n 39 at-bats with the Orioles in 1981, Cal Ripken Jr. failed to make much of an impression, hitting just .128. But he was Baltimore's Opening Day third baseman on April 5, 1982, and made a huge splash by going 3–for–5, including a two-run home run in his first at-bat. He would go on to win the American League Rookie of the Year Award. This article originally appeared on April 6, 1982.

# Ripken's Rookie Season Off to a Flying Start

The area around third base is a hallowed piece of real estate at Memorial Stadium.

Sure, it looks like any other third base in baseball. But Brooks Robinson didn't play everywhere else. Robby's Hall of Fame career set the standard upon which every Oriole third baseman will be judged.

"Everyone who plays third will be compared to Brooks Robinson," the Orioles' new third baseman, Cal Ripken Jr., said after the Birds routed Kansas City 13–5 in the American League's opener Monday.

"It's only natural. There's no doubt that Brooks was the best third baseman who's ever played. Not just on the Orioles. He was the best who ever played baseball.

"People will always say, 'That's a play that Brooks used to make.' It's extra pressure if I think about it."

Getting his first full season off to a good start was on Calvin Edwin Ripken's mind Monday. The 21-year-old, whose father, Cal Sr., is the Orioles' third-base coach, was 3–for–5 with a two-run homer in his first at-bat.

Ripken hit a Dennis Leonard fastball well over the wall in left field to give the Orioles a 2–1 lead in the second inning.

"I was very excited when I saw the ball go over the wall," Ripken said. "I could have jumped up and down all the way around the bases. I couldn't stop running. I ran real fast and caught up to Ken Singleton [who had walked to lead off the inning]."

By now, the media crush was closing in on Ripken. Locker room neighbor Mike Flanagan couldn't even see his belongings.

"You'll have to explain to my wife why I'm late," Flanagan said from behind the pack. "I want a new locker. Put me over near [pitcher Tim] Stoddard [who was on the 21-day disabled list]."

Ripken's pale blue eyes surveyed the crowd. He was sitting on a stool with all kinds of microphones, cameras, and notebooks thrust toward him. Hitting a Dennis Leonard fastball seemed easier than all this.

"I just don't know what to think about all this," Ripken said. "I'm at a loss for words. It's like World Series time. Isn't it? Is it worse than this at the World Series?" Assured that it was worse, Ripken just shook his head.

## Did You Know?

Ripken's first major league home run came off Kansas City's Dennis Leonard in the Orioles' Opening Day victory on April 5, 1982.

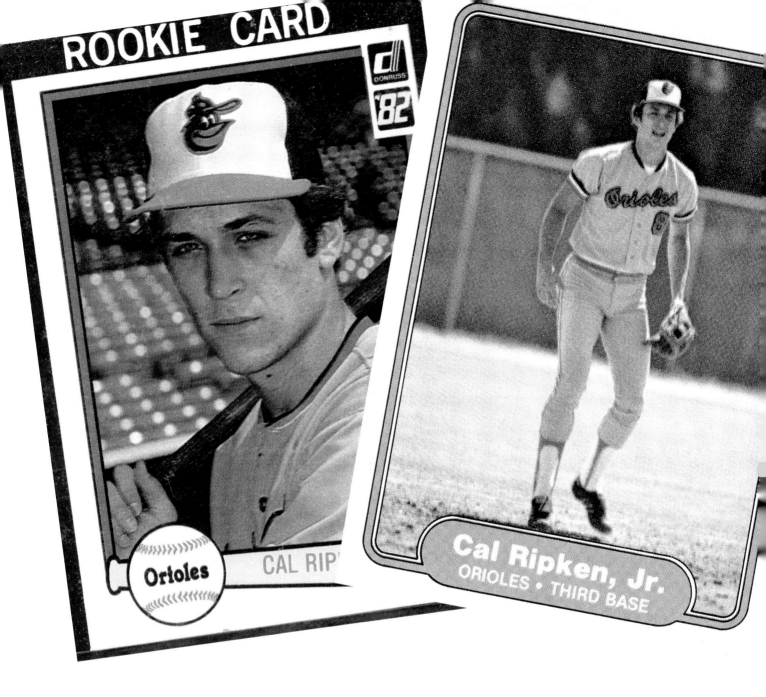

ROOKIE CARD

DONRUSS '82

Orioles    CAL RIP

Cal Ripken, Jr.
ORIOLES • THIRD BASE

Shaking your head is a lot better than having somebody after your head. Last September, a few people were calling for Ripken's scalp.

He came up from the Orioles' Triple A team in Rochester. He played in 23 unspectacular games with the O's, batting all of .128. He didn't hit any home runs. He didn't even drive in a run.

This from a 6'4", 200-pound kid whose father was a lifelong baseball man. Cal Jr.

didn't learn to play baseball before he knew how to walk, but it was close.

"Last year's experience helped me get my feet wet," Ripken says now.

He may not have been saying that last September.

"I have something to show for last year," he said. "People got down on me last year. They felt I wasn't the right guy for the job. People couldn't see what I can do."

**Orioles 13, Royals 5**

| KC | ab | r | h | bi | BAL | ab | r | h | bi |
|---|---|---|---|---|---|---|---|---|---|
| Wilson lf | 3 | 0 | 0 | 0 | Bumbry cf | 4 | 1 | 2 | 1 |
| Poquette lf | 2 | 0 | 0 | 0 | Dempsey c | 4 | 1 | 1 | 0 |
| Wathan c | 4 | 0 | 0 | 0 | Ford rf | 5 | 2 | 3 | 3 |
| Brett 3b | 4 | 1 | 2 | 1 | Singleton dh | 2 | 2 | 0 | 0 |
| Aikens 1b | 3 | 0 | 0 | 0 | Murray 1b | 5 | 1 | 1 | 4 |
| Otis cf | 5 | 2 | 1 | 0 | Ripken 3b | 5 | 2 | 3 | 2 |
| McRae dh | 3 | 1 | 1 | 0 | Roenicke lf | 5 | 2 | 4 | 1 |
| Martin rf | 4 | 0 | 1 | 0 | Sakata ss | 3 | 1 | 1 | 0 |
| White 2b | 4 | 1 | 2 | 4 | Dauer 2b | 5 | 1 | 1 | 2 |
| Washington ss | 2 | 0 | 0 | 0 | | | | | |
| Total | 34 | 5 | 8 | 5 | Total | 38 | 13 | 16 | 13 |

| | | |
|---|---|---|
| Kansas City | 010 300 100 - 5 | |
| Baltimore | 025 000 60x - 13 | |

E - Leonard. DP - Kansas City 2, Baltimore 1. LOB - Kansas City 9, Baltimore 8. 2B - Otis, Brett, Dauer, Ripken. HR - Ripken (1), Murray (1), Roenicke (1), White (1), Brett (1), Ford (1).

| Kansas City | IP | H | R | ER | BB | SO |
|---|---|---|---|---|---|---|
| Leonard L, 0-1 | 2 1/3 | 6 | 7 | 6 | 2 | 0 |
| Splittorff | 4 | 5 | 2 | 2 | 3 | 1 |
| GJackson | 2/3 | 4 | 4 | 4 | 1 | 0 |
| Black | 1 | 1 | 0 | 0 | 0 | 1 |

| Baltimore | IP | H | R | ER | BB | SO |
|---|---|---|---|---|---|---|
| DMartinez | 4 | 6 | 4 | 4 | 3 | 2 |
| Stewart W, 1-0 | 5 | 2 | 1 | 1 | 4 | 1 |

DMartinez pitched to 2 batters in the 5th.
HBP - by Leonard (Sakata)
T - 2:56. A - 52,034.

**Cal Ripken Jr. had a big day on Opening Day, April 5, 1982.**

When the Orioles traded veteran third baseman Doug DeCinces to the Angels over the winter, they essentially gave Ripken the job, for better or for worse.

"If I really think about it, I could put pressure on myself," Ripken said. "I just want to go out and do my job."

Ripken did say there was a little pressure on his first at-bat.

"It was a relief when I got a hit," he said. "I don't know if you could tell, but my bat was shaking when the ball was coming."

Ripken Sr. was shaking, also, when he saw his son's blast leave the ballpark.

Somehow he managed not to rush out to greet his son between first and second base, but waited at third.

"Nice hit, kid," he said. ■

*A*fter going 54–107 in 1988, the Orioles made some big changes in the off-season, including trading first baseman Eddie Murray to the Los Angeles Dodgers. But they brought back Cal Ripken Jr., signing him to a three-year contract. Ripken responded by leading the Orioles to a 5½-game lead in the AL East at the 1989 All-Star break. And Ripken went to Anaheim, California, for his sixth straight All-Star appearance. This story appeared on July 11, 1989.

Cal Ripken Sr., center, is flanked by sons Billy, left, and Cal Jr. at the Baltimore Orioles training camp in Miami, Florida, in February, 1987.
AP Photo/Joe Skipper

# Ho-Hum, Just Another Star in Ripken's Cap

Perhaps he's just too consistent, too good for even his own public relations.

Just because Cal Ripken Jr. starts his sixth straight All-Star Game tonight doesn't mean anyone will take notice. At this point in his career, Ripken is a bit like Niagara Falls: a sight to behold, but one so entrenched in people's minds that they pass him over for something more exotic.

Even this season, his own teammate has upstaged him. Although Ripken was the leading American League shortstop from the start, catcher Mickey Tettleton has been the subject of most All-Star stories connected with the Orioles. There's even been talk about the omissions of pitchers Jeff Ballard and Gregg Olson from the American League team.

But with Ripken, there's no controversy about his selection. And no argument.

"Sure, it's always an honor to go," he said. "I think everyone wants to go in some cases. I think if you've ever been to an All-Star Game, you have a real want or a need to go back. And I think it creates a little anxiety for [the] next year."

The All-Star break is a traditional yard-stick in baseball, and this year's measures up fine for Ripken.

**Ripken is where he wants to be. He plays for the only baseball team the Ripken family has known.**

After all, the 1989 season loomed as his biggest test since he was a rookie seven years ago.

So much had changed.

First, as the Orioles rebuilt from last year's 54–107 season, they toyed with moving Ripken to third base.

That coincided with a general housecleaning that purged all other high-profile veterans. To Ripken, Eddie Murray's absence was the most conspicuous, since Murray batted behind him. That cushion was gone when the Orioles dealt Murray to the Dodgers in December, only months after Ripken signed a three-year contract.

Ripken's decision to sign, much like the Orioles' maneuverings, was something of a risk. A chance. Or so it would seem to all but Ripken.

The club is in first place by 5½ games, but Ripken would still feel OK about his decision to stay, regardless of the Orioles' record.

"Obviously you have to feel better about the decision, being where you are. Everyone wants to be in first place and competitive. That wasn't supposed to happen so fast," he said.

However, he continued, "There was a lot more to my decision than being in first place this year.

"Probably, I felt I was young enough to withstand a rebuilding process. Secondly, I had already participated in a world championship team [1983]. The void was filled somewhat."

Ripken is where he wants to be. He plays for the only baseball team the Ripken family has known. Moreover, he's a fixture at shortstop, at least for the time being.

At the break, Ripken is hitting .275 with 11 home runs and 51 RBIs. If his average stays the same, and the power numbers are multiplied by two, then Ripken will have another status-quo season. When and if he hits home run No. 20, he will be the first-ever shortstop to have eight straight 20-homer seasons. He and Ernie Banks are the only ones to do it seven straight times.

Ripken said it's awkward to discuss offense in the context of being a shortstop.

Cal keeps the tag on Toronto's Alex Gonzalez as he is thrown out attempting to steal third base on June 19, 2001.

"To me, there's offense and defense," he said. "It's hard for me to grasp the concept of the shortstop hitting 20 home runs for eight years. Just because you play shortstop, it's hard for me to grasp the concept of the two."

But still, there's no rule that a club's third baseman must hit like Mike Schmidt and its shortstop like Mark Belanger.

Playing shortstop requires intense concentration. Ripken likes that. But that doesn't mean he'd ever doubt his ability to move to third base.

"The way I have success, if I'm doing my job right, it looks very boring."

"I enjoy [shortstop] probably the most only because of the responsibility that goes along with it," he said. "In my opinion, the pitcher and catcher are the people that are the busiest and have the most responsibility because they are involved in every pitch. Pitcher No. 1 and catcher No. 2. After that, the shortstop."

Ripken remains as modest as a struggling rookie—maybe because he was one early in the 1982 season. He's happy to see the Orioles in first place, but it won't affect his behavior at the All-Star Game or during the second half.

"I guess it'll give you a little more bragging rights to the other players. The All-Star Game is a game itself that doesn't really reflect too much what happens during the season," he said. ■

*al Ripken Jr. has always prided himself on his defense. In 1990, he set an all-time standard for consistency at shortstop by committing only three errors in 161 games, a .996 fielding percentage. It wasn't until after the 1991 season, however, that Ripken won the first of his two Gold Glove Awards. He won his second for his play in the 1992 season. The following story appeared on November 27, 1991.*

# O's Ripken Finally Strikes Gold

This one might've been the sweetest.

Cal Ripken, the American League Most Valuable Player, continued his sweep of the postseason awards on Tuesday by winning his first Rawlings Gold Glove Award.

The Orioles' shortstop also won Player of the Year honors from *The Sporting News* and the *Associated Press*. When he won his second MVP last week, Ripken said that although he coveted a Gold Glove, the desire was something he could control.

"Part of being successful at the big league level is winning a Gold Glove, and a small part of me has always wanted to win one," said Ripken. "I was hopeful I would get it one of these days. I've had a few years that I thought were good enough to win, but I've never been recognized for it.

"I could've accepted it if I didn't win because it wouldn't have diminished my accomplishments. But it feels awfully good to get one."

In 1990, Ripken had the best year of any shortstop, committing only three errors, but was beaten out by Chicago's Ozzie Guillen. Ripken, once uncomfortable talking about awards, admitted he felt slighted.

There was considerable backlash—Texas manager Bobby Valentine said he "was embarrassed" for the voters—which Ripken thought brought attention to his skills.

"Last year, I made three errors in the whole season and received a lot of attention for that, and there was some controversy surrounding the award," said Ripken. "I think maybe that heightened the awareness that maybe I should deserve some consideration."

This year, he led all major league shortstops in putouts (267), assists (529), chances (807), double plays (114), and fielding percentage. He committed only 11 errors. There was little doubt he'd win.

"There have been a lot of great moments," said Ripken of his career. "Perhaps the best was being part of the championship team in '83. Individually, to be recognized as a Gold Glove winner has to rank right up there.

"I've always been branded as an offensive player. . . . The defense was always overlooked. It's an area that I've had to work very hard at. I came up as a third baseman and I moved to shortstop and had to learn the position at the big league level. Winning that Gold Glove makes me feel really proud of the hard work I've put in." ■

*On July 19, 1991, Cal Ripken Jr. played in his 1,500th consecutive game, against the Seattle Mariners at Baltimore's Memorial Stadium. Just days earlier, he had been named MVP of the All-Star Game after going 2–for–3 and hitting a three-run home run in Toronto. This story appeared on July 20, 1991.*

# Cal Homers as The Streak Hits 1,500

Cal Ripken Jr. isn't playing as much as he used to.

Ripken, who was relieved at shortstop just 19 times in his first nine full seasons with the Baltimore Orioles, has been lifted 10 times this season alone.

But it's not like Ripken is showing any signs of his 30 years and 11 months of age.

Friday, against the Seattle Mariners, Ripken played in his 1,500th consecutive game, second only to Lou Gehrig on the all-time list. Before the game, the American League's leading hitter was presented with the 1991 All-Star Game MVP trophy, which he earned for hitting a three-run home run to give the American League a 4–2 win.

Then he went out and hit his 20th home run of the season.

Ripken has played 13,549 of a possible 13,633 innings since the consecutive-game streak began on May 30, 1982. He says he's not ready for a day off yet, but conceded before yesterday's game that he's glad to get a break every once in a while.

"As you get older, you find ways to get days off without getting days off," Ripken said. "Strategically, you might miss batting practice

or you might take a couple of days off from taking ground balls, just when you feel you might need it.

"At this level, I don't need to take batting practice every single day. It's just a matter of doing it to stay sharp. I can handpick those times."

Ripken had played nearly every inning since the streak began, but he's getting occasional breathers this season in the late innings of lop-sided games.

"I'll have to admit, when blowout games come, it's a pretty good mental break to take an inning off or two innings off when the game's out of hand," Ripken said. "I find that that's been useful."

Ripken has always shrugged off the significance of The Streak.

"I don't really try to downplay it," he said. "It's my way to deal with it. I don't keep track of it. I try to stay focused and play it one game at a time, the way you're supposed to."

"Sometimes, in a moment of weakness, you reflect upon it. But as a good practice, I just try to put it out of my mind, and say, 'You can't think about it. You've got too much baseball ahead of you.'"

Ripken would reach Gehrig's record of 2,130 consecutive games during the 1995 season.

"I don't plan to pace myself. I don't plan to skip anything that would allow me to play longer," he said. "It would be a mistake. You approach the game the same way all the time." ■

*On Sunday, June 6, 1993, the Baltimore Orioles and the Seattle Mariners got into a brawl at the Kingdome in Seattle. Ripken twisted his right knee during the mayhem and the injury almost brought an end to his consecutive-games streak. This article, published on June 12, 1993, describes one of Ripken's closest calls.*

# Cal Almost Ended The Streak

For a couple of hours Monday morning, The Streak was in jeopardy.

According to one newspaper report, Cal Ripken slightly twisted his right knee during Sunday's brawl against the Seattle Mariners, and he briefly considered the possibility of not playing when it stiffened overnight.

Had he taken himself out of the lineup, The Streak would have ended at 1,790 games.

"Is this really a big deal?" Ripken asked reporters before Friday's game against Boston at Fenway Park.

Ripken's health certainly didn't appear to be an issue after the brawl; he didn't limp when play resumed and he participated in batting and infield practice all week. Also, Orioles manager Johnny Oates reported that the only injuries in the brawl were Jeff Tackett's black eye and Mark Williamson's bruised nose.

Ripken said his knee tightened overnight, but responded to ice treatments Monday. He decided to play when his knee didn't bother him after infield and batting practice.

"I twisted my knee and the next day it was stiff and it was difficult to do anything," Ripken said. "It didn't seem feasible to run around on it. It seemed serious at the time, and since I've never had a knee injury before, I didn't know."

Before he went to the park Monday, he mentioned the possibility of sitting out to his wife, Kelly.

"My wife said, 'Do you think it's possible to play one inning tonight?' and I said, 'You too?'" Ripken said. "She said, 'I thought that's what is important to you,' and I said, 'If I can't play, I'm not willing to play.'"

The closest Ripken has come to not playing was early in the 1985 season, when he twisted an ankle in a Wednesday game against the Texas Rangers. He missed an exhibition game the next day against the Naval Academy, but played on that Friday.

Had Thursday been a regular-season game, Ripken wouldn't have played and The Streak would not have been. ■

"To play as demanding a position as he does and to play as well as he does is unbelievable. He has got to be as strong mentally as anybody who has ever played this game."
—*longtime Detroit Tigers shortstop Alan Trammell*

*On August 1, 1994, Ripken played his 2,000th consecutive game, at the Metrodome in Minneapolis, Minnesota. Fewer than two weeks later, major league players went on strike, ending the 1994 season and forcing Ripken to wait a little longer in his pursuit of Lou Gehrig's record. This article originally appeared on August 2, 1994.*

# After 2,000 Games, Ripken Says He's Getting Comfortable

Cal Ripken said it was no big deal. He said it was like any other game.

Only this routine game had reporters flying in from around the country.

Only this routine game began with a prolonged standing ovation from the opposing crowd, which required two tips of the hat to acknowledge.

Only this routine game had his wife, Kelly, flying in from Baltimore to surprise him.

Monday night's routine game in the Metrodome was Ripken's 2,000th straight, leaving him 130 shy of Lou Gehrig's all-time record.

"I try to downplay it as best as I can," Ripken said.

When Ripken moved past Everett Scott and into second place in 1990, he was defensive

when asked if he thought his career would be defined by The Streak.

"I think that might be a little unfair, because I've been able to accomplish some other things," Ripken said at the time.

To be fair, he had.

Ripken was the 1982 Rookie of the Year. He won a World Championship in 1983 and was the American League MVP. He had a string of consecutive 20-plus homer seasons.

"There are times when you have those little nagging injuries. There are days when you just don't feel well. For him to play so many games in a row and not get seriously injured playing at shortstop is just unbelievable."
—*York, Pennsylvania, resident Marlyn Holtzapple, a former minor league baseball player*

He's also added an understanding of how he's perceived.

When asked again if it was fair that The Streak defines his career, Ripken said: "I'm comfortable with that. . . . I know that's part of my identity. Over the years, getting asked about it every day, I think I've matured a little bit. I understand that it's a part of me. It's taken a while for me to understand it." ■

## Did You Know?

Just 18 major leaguers appeared in games in both 1982, when Ripken's streak began, and in 1998, when the streak ended. They were: Harold Baines, Rafael Belliard, Wade Boggs, Danny Darwin, Chili Davis, Dennis Eckersley, Jim Eisenreich, Gary Gaetti, Tony Gwynn, Rickey Henderson, Doug Jones, Dennis Martinez, Willie McGee, Paul Molitor, Jesse Orosco, Tony Phillips, Tim Raines, and Dave Stieb.

*If you're a Baltimore Orioles fan, you will always remember exactly where you were at 9:20 P.M. on Wednesday, September 6, 1995. That's when Cal Ripken Jr. officially passed Lou Gehrig's consecutive-games record and became baseball's new Iron Man. This article originally appeared on September 7, 1995.*

# 2,131: Cal Makes His Mark in History

As the Baltimore Orioles took the field Wednesday night, the players abruptly stopped and remained in the dugout to let Cal Ripken take his position alone.

Five innings later, he stood alone in baseball history.

At 9:20 P.M., when Manny Alexander caught Damion Easley's pop-up to end the fifth inning, Ripken's 2,131st consecutive game was official and the record held by New York Yankee Lou Gehrig for more than half a century had fallen.

The banner on the B&O Warehouse facade behind the right-field wall in Camden Yards was unfurled to reveal the number 2,131, and what followed was a thunderous 22-minute, 15-second standing ovation that culminated in Ripken circling the Camden Yards field shaking hands with fans and the entire California Angels team.

"When I was running around the fence, it became a whole lot more personal," Ripken said afterward. "It was like signing autographs. You could exchange greetings. You could shake hands. It was intimate. It was good."

While Baltimore fans cheered their favorite son, one sign was seen in the left-field stands: "Cal, Thanks for Saving Baseball."

That sentiment was shared by fans throughout the country as Ripken's ovation was telecast on scoreboards in major league stadiums. At Boston's Fenway Park, the game between the Boston Red Sox and the Oakland Athletics was delayed as fans and players, even pitcher Roger Clemens, who was on the mound at the time, stopped to cheer Ripken.

Ripken's assault on history began on May 30, 1982, when he was a rookie third baseman. Watching him finally finish with the record were his family, including his father Cal Sr., a former Orioles coach and manager, and brother Billy, a teammate from 1987–1992. Also on hand were President Bill Clinton and Vice President Al Gore, acting commissioner Bud Selig, and numerous celebrities from the world of entertainment and sports, most notably Yankees Hall of Famer Joe DiMaggio, a teammate of Gehrig's.

"Cal Ripken, in a funny way, because of this achievement, has made people stop and recognize the common worker," Clinton told a national television audience.

Ripken's playing reputation is that of fundamental consistency and his persona has always been quiet and reserved. However, on his biggest night, he again demonstrated a flair for the dramatic with a tremendous home run

# Did You Know?

There were several moments that almost ended Ripken's consecutive-games streak:

- April 10, 1985, Game 444: Ripken sprained his left ankle during a pickoff play against Texas. He did not play in an exhibition game the next day but was in the lineup vs. Toronto the day after that.

- September 11, 1992, Game 1,713: Ripken twisted his right ankle running out a double against Milwaukee. He finished the game. Baltimore recalled Manny Alexander from Rochester as a precaution, but Ripken did not miss an inning for more than a week.

- June 6, 1993, Game 1,790: Ripken twisted his right knee during a melee between the Orioles and the Mariners. He finished the game, and although the knee was swollen and painful the next day, he took infield practice and started the game. "It was the closest I've come to not playing," he would later say.

- August 2, 1997, Game 2,423: Ripken considered leaving the game in the bottom of the first at Oakland due to lower back pain. He remained in the game, singled in his next at-bat, and homered the next day.

# Sports Illustrated

Sportsman
of the Year
CAL RIPKEN JR.

The December 18, 1995, cover of *Sports Illustrated*,
which named Cal Ripken Jr. its "Sportsman of the Year."

in the fourth inning, his 15th of the season, the 325th of his career, and his third in three games.

Ripken always maintained The Streak was built on luck and skill, but it was mostly a creation of the iron-willed work ethic instilled by his father. Throughout the past 14 summers, Ripken insisted he played out of desire, love of the sport, and quite simply because it was his job.

Never, Ripken said, did he play for the record.

"The Streak is something I'm proud of, but I can honestly say I never played to continue The Streak," he said recently. "I never set out to do this. I'm a baseball player and I was taught the importance of being in the lineup every day. To me, The Streak is an extension of my approach and my beliefs."

That approach survived ankle sprains in 1985 and 1992, a twisted right knee in 1993, numerous bruises, jammed fingers, and various aches. Ripken played tired, against all pitchers, and under all conditions, but nothing kept him out of the lineup.

The most serious threat to Ripken's streak came this spring. During the eight-month strike by the Major League Baseball Players Association, the owners threatened to open the season with replacement players.

Although Ripken could have played alongside replacements to extend The Streak, he steadfastly refused to break the strike line and always said he was willing to let The Streak end. The issue became a moot point when the players and owners signed a back-to-work agreement. The Streak resumed April 26 in Kansas City at 2,009 games, 122 shy of Gehrig.

It has been a tumultuous season in baseball with attendance down by more than 20 percent. However, the attention given Ripken and The Streak seem to have overcome that bitterness. ∎

"The Streak is something I'm proud of, but I can honestly say I never played to continue The Streak. I never set out to do this. I'm a baseball player and I was taught the importance of being in the lineup every day."
—Cal Ripken Jr.

*The scene at Camden Yards on September 6, 1995, was amazing, as 46,272 fans gathered to celebrate Cal Ripken Jr.'s 2,131st consecutive game. This September 7, 1995, piece describes the fans' jubilation.*

# They Were There to Watch Cal, Not the Game

Nobody came to Oriole Park at Camden Yards Wednesday night for the Orioles game against the California Angels. The crowd of 46,272 came to be a part of sports history.

"The game's a dud," said Bob Coleman, a Hanover, Pennsylvania, resident who, with his wife, Joan, owns an amazing collection of Cal Ripken memorabilia. "We're not here for the game. Nobody's here for the game."

It didn't matter whether the Orioles won or lost. The fans were here to see Calvin Edwin Ripken Jr. eclipse a baseball record that nobody thought would ever be broken, the streak of consecutive games played set by the great Yankee first baseman Lou Gehrig.

Wednesday night, Ripken played his 2,131st straight game.

The scene at the ballpark was unlike anything anyone had ever seen. Veterans of All-Star games, World Series games, any event, all said it was nothing like they'd ever seen.

"I didn't think it'd be anything like this," Glenn Zumbrum Jr., a Spring Grove, Pennsylvania, native and lifelong Orioles fan, said as he surveyed the huge crowd clogging the concourse.

The fans were primed. They cheered wildly when Ripken was introduced.

# Did You Know?

During Ripken's consecutive-games streak, the Dow Jones Industrial Average rose more than 7,000 points, from 819.54 to 7,895.66.

Ripken bats during his record-breaking game, No. 2,131, on September 6, 1995.

They cheered wildly when he took to the field to stretch before the game.

They went nuts when his five-year-old daughter, Rachel, and two-year-old son, Ryan, threw out the ceremonial first pitches.

They went crazy when Ripken hit a home run in the fourth inning.

They went absolutely nuts in the middle of the fifth inning, when the game became official and a banner was unfurled on the B&O Warehouse to raise the Cal count to 2,131.

The game was delayed for 22 minutes and 15 seconds while fans showered Ripken with unconditional love.

Even the Angels players on the field applauded.

The umpires applauded.

Ripken responded by jogging around the field, shaking fans' hands.

In the stands, Cal's wife, Kelly, wiped tears from her eyes. His mother, Vi, wept. Cal's father, former Oriole manager Cal Sr., stood stoically. That's just the way he is.

"Amazing," one fan said. "Utterly amazing."

The only sour spot was when President Clinton was shown on the stadium's large-screen TV. The fans interrupted their love-fest to boo briefly. Maybe it was political: a fan in left field held a banner aloft that said, "Cal For President."

But the fans saved the loudest cheers of the night for the emotional postgame ceremonies.

Fans began arriving at the ballpark early in the morning. By 11:00 A.M., fans filled the plaza outside the Eutaw Street entrance of Camden Yards, already forming a line to enter the gate even though it would not open for another five hours.

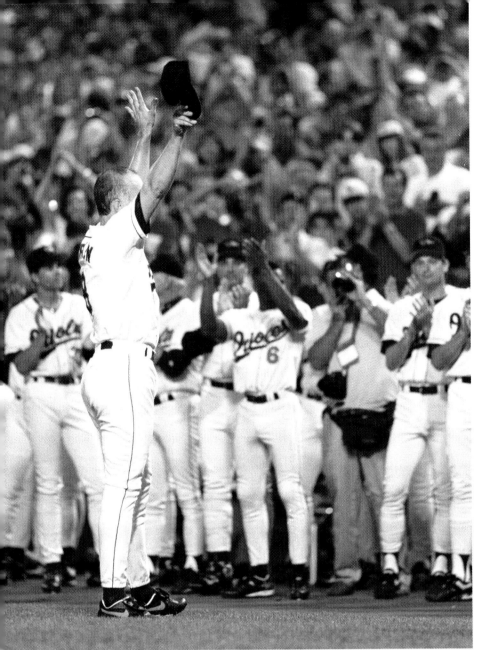

The 1,200 balls sold out in minutes and fans left waiting in line were given handouts that instructed them on how to order the $20 souvenir by mail.

An hour before game time, long lines remained for programs. Word had not spread yet that the programs had sold out long before, many grabbed by sports memorabilia collectors.

Among the fans who arrived early were the Colemans. They left their Hanover home at 7:30 A.M., taking their time driving to Baltimore. The chances that they'd miss this game were "between slim and none," Bob said.

Street hawkers did a brisk business, selling anything from caps to T-shirts to orange Cal Ripken rally towels. Anything with Cal Ripken and the number 2,131 sold well and quickly.

Once the gates opened, Eutaw Street between the B&O Warehouse and the stadium filled quickly, with fans forming long lines to buy programs and baseballs that were manufactured especially for the game. The balls bore Cal's signature and had orange laces instead of the traditional red.

The Colemans have arguably the world's most extensive collection of Cal Ripken memorabilia, owning between 7,000 and 9,000 different items. On the way to the ballpark Wednesday, they found a Crown gas station that was selling Cal Ripken commemorative Coke bottles and bought a six-pack of them.

They began collecting Cal stuff in 1988. Bob's father had been a big Ripken fan. When he died, they were combing through his baseball card collection when Joan found a Ripken

card. She mentioned it'd be neat to collect Ripken stuff.

"For $10, I can buy you every Ripken card ever made," Bob told her.

Now, Bob said, "Little did I know, it'd be more like 10,000 bucks."

The Colemans have been to spring training and Cal's winter festivals. They comb sports memorabilia shows, looking for Ripken collectibles.

"He's a role model in a time when people need role models," Bob said. "He's a family man. He's dedicated to his work and to his hometown. He's just a regular guy." ▪

## Did You Know?

Cal Ripken also holds what is believed to be a major league record for consecutive innings played, 8,243. The streak started on June 5, 1982, and ended on September 14, 1987, when manager Cal Ripken Sr. inserted Ron Washington at shortstop in the bottom of the eighth inning of an 18–3 Toronto win.

Lou Gehrig, first baseman of the New York Yankees, takes practice swings before the start of the 1932 World Series against the Chicago Cubs in New York City on September 16, 1932. Cal Ripken broke Gehrig's consecutive-games record on September 6, 1995. *AP Photo*

*In this story, published on September 7, 1995, one of Lou Gehrig's former teammates on the New York Yankees says Gehrig would have been the first to congratulate Cal Ripken Jr. for breaking his Iron Man streak.*

# Former Teammate: Gehrig Would Have Been Proud

If Tommy Henrich is right about his old teammate (and if that teammate were still alive), Cal Ripken's Baltimore teammates wouldn't have been the first to congratulate him for surpassing Lou Gehrig's consecutive-games record.

Gehrig himself would have.

"I think he'd want to be the first guy to congratulate Ripken because he's done it with such class," Henrich said recently from his home in Prescott, Arizona.

Henrich ought to know. He is one of only four living teammates of Gehrig's from Gehrig's final season with the 1939 New York Yankees.

Another Gehrig teammate, Hall of Famer Joe DiMaggio, was present to honor Ripken's accomplishment Wednesday night.

Henrich, now 82, believes Gehrig would have handled Ripken's pursuit of 2,130 straight games with the same grace and dignity he showed in his battle with amyotrophic lateral sclerosis.

"There was nothing in Lou Gehrig's personality that would imply to Cal Ripken, 'If I hadn't gotten [sick], you wouldn't have touched me. You wouldn't have come close.' No, Gehrig never would have said that. He was a high-class guy."

Henrich joined the Yankees in 1938, so his first two seasons were Gehrig's last.

"[We were] fairly close," Henrich said. "Don't forget there's a big difference in age. He was quite a veteran, but he was very kind to me. I enjoyed his company. He had a good sense of humor. I was naturally in awe of him."

Henrich still vividly remembers one of his first games with the Yankees, when a slumping Gehrig was dropped to sixth in the lineup against the Philadelphia Athletics.

"He got four line drives, four base hits," Henrich recalled. "I said to his real pal, Bill Dickey, 'My God, I've never seen such line drives in my life.'

"Dickey said, 'Stick around, Tommy. What you saw today were soft line drives.' I said, 'If those were soft ones, what the heck kind of guy is this?'"

Gehrig's best and healthiest days were behind him, though. During spring training of 1939, it was clear that something was wrong.

After hitting .143 in the season's first eight games, Gehrig asked Yankees manager Joe McCarthy to bench him.

Gehrig passed away a little more than two years after that, on June 2, 1941.

Like Ripken, Gehrig seldom brought up his consecutive-games streak, Henrich said.

"He was proud of it, but I don't think I ever heard him say something about his streak," he said. "He wasn't that kind of guy." ■

When the game numbers on the warehouse changed during fifth innings over the past several weeks, the fans in this ballpark responded incredibly. I'm not sure that my reactions showed how I really felt. I just didn't know what to do. Tonight, I want to make sure you know how I feel.

As I grew up here, I not only had dreams of being a big league ballplayer, but also of being a Baltimore Oriole. As a boy and a fan, I know how passionate we feel about baseball and the Orioles here. And as a player, I have benefited from this passion. For all of your support over the years, I want to thank you, the fans of Baltimore, from the bottom of my heart. This is the greatest place to play.

This year has been unbelievable. I've been cheered in ballparks all over the country. People not only showed me their kindness, but more importantly, they demonstrated their love of the game of baseball. I give my thanks to baseball fans everywhere.

I also could express my gratitude to a number of individuals who have played a role in my life and my career, but if I try to mention them all, I might unintentionally miss someone and take more time than I should.

There are, however, four people I want to thank specially. Let me start by thanking my dad. He inspired me with his commitment to the Orioles tradition and made me understand the importance of it. He not only taught me fundamentals of the game of baseball, but also taught me to play it the right way, and to play it the Oriole way. From the very beginning, my dad let me know how important it was to be there for your team and to be counted on by your teammates.

My mom. What can I say about my mom? She is an unbelievable person. She let my dad lead the way on the field, but she was there in every other way, leading and shaping the lives of our family off the field. She's the glue that held our lives together while we grew up, and she's always been my inspiration.

Dad and Mom laid the foundation for my baseball career and my life, and when I got to the big leagues, there was a man, Eddie

"At first it was overwhelming. And then it started to become personal. You started to see people in the stands that you recognized, started to see somebody you went to school with, and you started to see other people. Then I looked at the box and looked up at my dad. There was just a certain moment, no words had to be spoken."
—*Cal Ripken Jr. remembering the night he broke Lou Gehrig's record, during a 2001 interview*

One of the special baseballs made to commemorate Cal Ripken Jr. breaking Lou Gehrig's consecutive-games record.

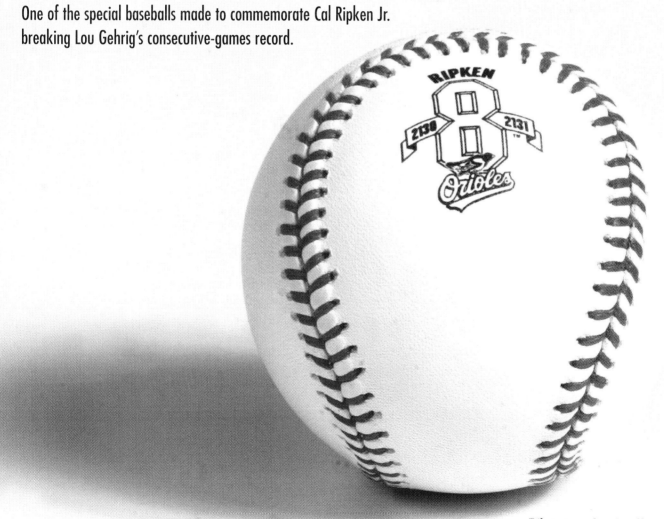

2131 1ST PITCHED BALL.

96.2.30.

The first pitched ball from Ripken's record-breaking 2,131st game.

Murray, who showed me how to play this game, day in and day out. I thank him for his example and for his friendship. I was lucky to have him as my teammate for the years we were together, and I congratulate him on the great achievement of 3,000 hits this year.

As my major league career moved along, the most important person came into my life, my wife Kelly. She has enriched it with her friendship and with her love. I thank you, Kelly, for the advice, support, and joy you have brought to me and for always being there. You, Rachel, and Ryan are my life.

These people, and many others, have allowed me, day in and day out, to play the great American game of baseball. Tonight I stand here, overwhelmed, as my name is linked with the great and courageous Lou Gehrig. I'm truly humbled to have our names spoken in the same breath. Some may think

Cal Ripken Jr. played in his 2,131st consecutive game and broke Lou Gehrig's record on September 6, 1995.

**Orioles 4, Angels 2**

| CAL | ab | r | h | bi | BAL | ab | r | h | bi |
|---|---|---|---|---|---|---|---|---|---|
| Phillips 3b | 4 | 0 | 0 | 0 | BAnderson cf | 4 | 0 | 1 | 0 |
| Edmonds cf | 3 | 1 | 1 | 0 | Alexander 2b | 4 | 0 | 0 | 0 |
| Salmon rf | 4 | 1 | 3 | 2 | RPalmeiro 1b | 4 | 2 | 3 | 2 |
| CDavis dh | 3 | 0 | 0 | 0 | Bonilla rf | 4 | 1 | 1 | 1 |
| Snow 1b | 4 | 0 | 1 | 0 | Brown rf | 0 | 0 | 0 | 0 |
| GAnderson lf | 4 | 0 | 0 | 0 | Ripken ss | 4 | 1 | 2 | 1 |
| Hudler 2b | 2 | 0 | 0 | 0 | Baines dh | 4 | 0 | 1 | 0 |
| Owen 2b | 2 | 0 | 0 | 0 | Hoiles c | 4 | 0 | 1 | 0 |
| Fabregas c | 3 | 0 | 0 | 0 | Huson 3b | 4 | 0 | 0 | 0 |
| Easley ss | 2 | 0 | 1 | 0 | Smith lf | 2 | 0 | 0 | 0 |
| OPalmeiro ph | 1 | 0 | 0 | 0 | | | | | |
| Correia ss | 0 | 0 | 0 | 0 | | | | | |
| Total | 32 | 2 | 6 | 2 | Total | 34 | 4 | 9 | 4 |

California   100 000 010 - 2
Baltimore    100 200 10x - 4

E - Phillips (15). DP - Baltimore 1. LOB - California 5, Baltimore 7. 2B - Salmon (28), Easley (11), Baines (13). 3B - Edmonds (2). HR - Salmon (32), RPalmeiro 2 (34), Bonilla (6), Ripken (15).

| California | IP | H | R | ER | BB | SO |
|---|---|---|---|---|---|---|
| Boskie L, 6-4 | 5 | 6 | 3 | 3 | 1 | 4 |
| Bielecki | 1 | 1 | 0 | 0 | 0 | 2 |
| BPatterson | 2/3 | 1 | 1 | 1 | 0 | 1 |
| James | 1 1/3 | 1 | 0 | 0 | 0 | 1 |

| Baltimore | IP | H | R | ER | BB | SO |
|---|---|---|---|---|---|---|
| Mussina W, 16-8 | 7 2/3 | 5 | 2 | 2 | 2 | 7 |
| TClark | 0 | 1 | 0 | 0 | 0 | 0 |
| Orosco S, 1 | 1 1/3 | 0 | 0 | 0 | 0 | 2 |

TClark pitched to 1 batter in the 8th.
Umpires - Home, Barnett; First, Kosc; Second, Morrison; Third, Clark.
T - 3:35. A - 46,272.

our strongest connection is because we have both played many consecutive games. Yet I believe in my heart that our true link is a common motivation—a love of the game of baseball, a passion for our team, and a desire to compete on the very highest level.

I know that if Lou Gehrig is looking down on tonight's activities, he isn't concerned about someone playing one more consecutive game than he did. Instead, he's viewing tonight as just another example of what is good and right about the great American game.

Whether your name is Gehrig or Ripken, DiMaggio or Robinson, or that of some youngster who picks up his bat or puts on his glove, you are challenged by the game of baseball to do your very best day in and day out. And that's all I've ever tried to do. Thank you. ■

*On September 20, 1998, at Camden Yards, about 30 minutes before the Orioles' final home game of the season, baseball's all-time Iron Man asked manager Ray Miller to remove him from the starting lineup. The Streak was over. The final tally: 2,632 consecutive games. This story was published on Monday, September 21, 1998, the day after The Streak ended.*

# Finally, Cal Gets a Day Off

Ripken waves to the crowd prior to a game against the New York Yankees at Camden Yards Sunday, September 20, 1998. Ripken sat the game out, ending his record consecutive-games streak at 2,632. *AP Photo/John Gillis*

The world didn't end, but another part of it you thought could never change just did.

Your sky is still blue, your clouds are still white, and, in Baltimore, the Sun still towers over Camden Yards. But over in that most sacred piece of the park—that little patch of dirt where you knew who you were going to see night after night after night—a piece of America just became history.

Cal Ripken Jr. missed a baseball game.

Blink. Read it again.

Cal Ripken Jr. missed a baseball game.

He figured this all out on Thursday, although it was a plan he had been thinking about since June.

Rest easy, America. Your hero was not hurt. He went out on his own terms, in front of his own people.

The 48,013 fans at Camden Yards, still trying to let it all sink in, gave Cal a standing ovation.

He came out of the dugout and was a boy, a boy finally skipping school after 2,632 straight days without playing hooky.

Oh, he had that shy grin as he waved to the Yankees and waved to the crowd. Oh, it was like Streak Night, back when he broke Lou Gehrig's record of 2,130 games on September 6, 1995.

But this wasn't Streak Night. This was The End.

On the other hand, it's just the end of The Streak, that's all.

Man, Cal wanted everyone to know that. He wanted them to stop worrying. He wanted the little kids to wipe their tears, wanted to calm their parents' fears.

"I wanted to tell everyone, 'It's OK,' " he said. "To scream and yell as loud as I could, 'It's not a sad moment,' " he continued, smiling. "I'm not gonna sit here and bawl my eyes out. I'll do that later."

But he couldn't scream above these fans, couldn't tell them not to bawl their eyes out. So he did the next best thing. He looked at starting pitcher Doug Johns and waved at him to pitch.

"Contrary to some reports that I'm on my last breath, I feel that I'm an everyday player and that I still have a lot of baseball left in me," he said. "This isn't going to change my approach."

Sure, he'll be open to sitting down a couple of times next year. He'll think about it. He just won't like it.

"Now that I know what it feels like, I don't want to sit around and watch," he said. "I was very antsy and fidgety."

It was simply, as he told manager Ray Miller shortly before the game, "the right time."

"If this is gonna end, let it end in front of the best fans in baseball," he said in a postgame press conference full of reporters who came streaming into Camden Yards throughout the night. "This isn't a sad thing. I wanted it to be a festive, happy thing."

For the most part, it was. The visiting New York Yankees gathered at the top step of their dugout and tipped their caps and applauded.

He made the most of his day off, visiting reliever Alan Mills in the bullpen and playing catch with left fielder B. J. Surhoff before the top of the sixth.

Ripken said he's known since June that it was time. He thought, at first, that he would just sit out the last game of the season at Boston, but decided to end it where it began, at home. That way the fans could celebrate with him.

He told his wife, Kelly, who looked like she was still trying to deal with The End at a postgame press conference.

"How are you?" Cal asked her.

She shot him a look.

"I'll tell you later," she said.

He told his dad, Cal Sr., and his mother, Vi.

They asked him why he wanted to do it and accepted his decision, as he expected.

He didn't want to distract from the team anymore. He was getting uncomfortable with that. And now that the season was almost over, might as well get it out of the way.

"I don't feel a sense of relief," Ripken said at the packed postgame press conference.

In the background, a tiny TV camera showed Ripken's face. Underneath, a graphic said, "Cal ends streak."

"I don't feel much different really," Ripken added.

But now everything is different.

The world hasn't ended, but we've lost another part of it. Your sky is still blue, your clouds are still white, but something felt just a little off Sunday night.

Cal Ripken Jr. missed a baseball game.

Blink. Read it again.

Cal Ripken Jr. missed a baseball game. ■

## Did You Know?

Ripken is one of only two shortstops (Chicago Cubs Hall of Famer Ernie Banks was the other) selected to Major League Baseball's All-Century Team, which was voted on by fans and a panel of experts in 1999.

*T*his September 21, 1998, piece offers a taste of the reaction of fans who were at Camden Yards when Cal Ripken Jr.'s consecutive-games streak finally came to an end.

# Fans in Shock that The Streak Is Over

Brian Killefer and his brother looked at the Orioles lineup on the scoreboard.

They looked again.

They couldn't believe it.

It was still there: 3B Ryan Minor.

The Orioles lineup was on the scoreboard. And for the first time in 2,632 games and 16 years, Cal Ripken Jr.'s name wasn't included.

"I was dumbfounded," Killefer, a 32-year-old Baltimore resident, said. "It's been a constant for 15 years. You don't look at the lineup . . . it's ridiculous."

Shortly before the game, Ripken pulled manager Ray Miller aside and asked him to keep his name out of the lineup.

"I think the time is right," Ripken told him.

Right or not, the timing shocked Ripken's teammates, fans, and friends.

"It's a strange thing," said Claudia Smigrod, a 48-year-old from Alexandria, Virginia. "It's a very strange thing, isn't it? It doesn't even feel right, does it?"

It didn't feel right for ten-year-old Jeffrey Israel, who sat behind the Orioles dugout. He did what a lot of children would have done.

He cried.

"Why'd you cry?" his father, Richard, asked him later.

Jeffrey looked at his father like he was a fool.

"Because Cal didn't play," he said. "Why else?"

But maybe he still would, some fans thought. Maybe he would pinch hit or play defense and keep The Streak—the one that surpassed Lou Gehrig's streak of 2,130 consecutive games on September 6, 1995—alive.

As the game progressed, though, and Ripken made good on his promise to visit reliever Alan Mills in the bullpen, the fans started to realize that this was it.

Cal had decided to end The Streak at home.

"I can't believe it's over," said Ken Valentine of Chester, Maryland.

Neither could all the fans waiting in long lines for the programs that would sell out before the end of the game.

The answer to why they were waiting was as simple as the answer to why Jeffrey cried.

"Why? Why?" Janie Greiss of York said. "Why does everyone else want one? Because Cal sat down." ■

Ripken sits in the dugout at the start of the game against the New York Yankees at Camden Yards in Baltimore on Sunday, September 20, 1998. Ripken, who had started in 2,632 consecutive games since May 30, 1982, broke his major league record streak by sitting out of this game. *AP Photo/John Gillis*

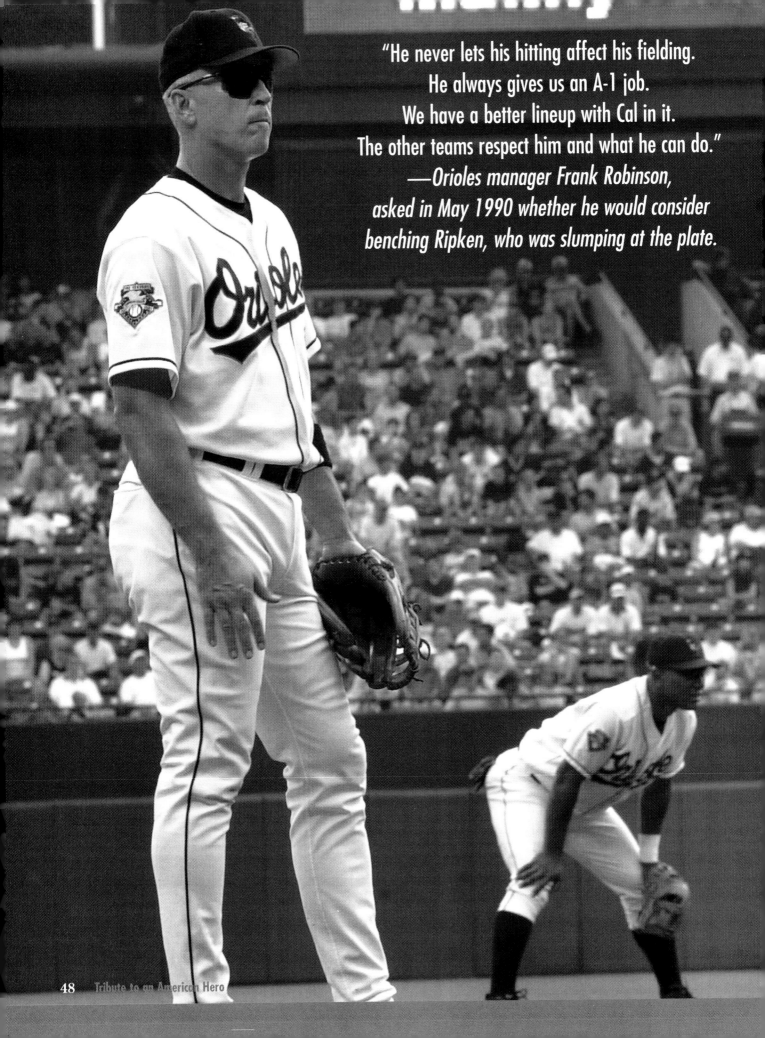

"He never lets his hitting affect his fielding.
He always gives us an A-1 job.
We have a better lineup with Cal in it.
The other teams respect him and what he can do."
—Orioles manager Frank Robinson,
asked in May 1990 whether he would consider
benching Ripken, who was slumping at the plate.

*On December 12, 1996, the Baltimore Orioles signed free-agent shortstop Mike Bordick, sealing their plans to move Cal Ripken Jr. back to his original position at third base. The move could certainly be called a success, as Ripken and Bordick helped lead the Orioles to their second consecutive American League Championship Series in 1997. The following story was published on December 13, 1996.*

## Cal's Career Turns Corner

There's another chapter in the Cal Ripken Jr. Hall of Fame story.

"The Third Base Years, Part II" began Thursday night when the Baltimore Orioles, after weeks of speculation, signed free-agent shortstop Mike Bordick.

Ripken has been a fixture at shortstop throughout most of his career. The Orioles did try a similar move 10 years ago, an ill-fated mistake now known as the Juan Bell experiment. Of course, back in 1990, when Ripken made only three errors all season long at baseball's most demanding position, moving him would have been unthinkable. Last summer, when manager Davey Johnson hinted at the switch and later moved Ripken for six games, it caused quite a firestorm. But the move became a reality on December 12 when Bordick signed a three-year deal worth $9 million with an option for a fourth year.

In announcing the signing, Orioles general manager Pat Gillick took great pains not to

## Did You Know?

As a member of the Rochester Red Wings in 1981, Ripken was a participant in the longest game in baseball history. The Red Wings and the Pawtucket Red Sox began what would be a 33-inning game on April 18, 1981, and resumed and completed the game on June 23, 1981, with Pawtucket finally winning, 3–2. The total time of the game was eight hours and 25 minutes. Ripken played third base for the Red Wings, batted third, and went 2–for–13. Among the other future major leaguers appearing in the game were Marty Barrett, Wade Boggs, Rich Gedman, Floyd Rayford, Bruce Hurst, and Bob Ojeda.

slight Ripken and thanked the 14-time All-Star for his cooperation.

"I think Cal did a great job for us at shortstop this year. This doesn't mean we think Cal can't play shortstop any longer. We believe this makes us a better team.

"We're extremely excited to add Mike to our infield. He is one of the premier shortstops in the American League, and with Cal Ripken at third base, it gives us a very strong left side of the infield. I don't think many balls will get between Cal and Mike. This move already makes our pitching better by making us a better defensive team."

Ripken broke into the majors at the end of the 1981 season playing both third base and shortstop, and opened his Rookie of the Year season in 1982 at third base. He played regularly at third until June 30 of that year, when Hall of Fame manager Earl Weaver moved him to shortstop for the following game.

Ripken made 2,216 consecutive starts at shortstop until this year, when Johnson moved him to third base for six games starting July 15.

Not just any player could replace Ripken, who holds or shares 11 major league or

Ripken kidding around with his teammates.

American League shortstop fielding records, and whose stature in the clubhouse and steady presence in the field could be overwhelming to the timid.

Bordick, 31, is a career .258 hitter in seven seasons with the Oakland Athletics; last season he led American League shortstops with 476 assists and was second in total chances (757) and double plays (121).

There isn't much doubt Bordick can play the position. The only doubt was whether he'd be able to play it in Baltimore. That question seemingly was answered in the positive on Wednesday night when Bordick talked with Ripken.

Bordick said the purpose of the call wasn't to solicit Ripken's blessing. Instead, he wanted to be sure that he wouldn't be the root of a divided clubhouse in 1997.

"He's a great team player," said Bordick, speaking from his Auburn, Maine, off-season home. "And, if it happened where he had to move to third base, I think he'd do it to help the team."

"Without Cal's cooperation, this wouldn't have gotten done," Gillick added. "Cal played a very instrumental role in getting this accomplished. Cal got a taste of the postseason this year and wants to go back, and I think he believes this makes us a better team." ■

*The year 1997 was a difficult one for Cal Ripken Jr. He made 22 errors in his first year back at third base. He hit just .270 with 17 home runs. His back ached for weeks and weeks. But in the end Ripken added another 162 games to his consecutive-games streak and batted .385 in the postseason; the Orioles knocked off Seattle and then took Cleveland to six games before losing in the American League Championship Series. This column was published on October 4, 1997, after Ripken and the Orioles won the first two games of their playoff series against the Mariners.*

# Ripken Responds by Wearing Out Mariners

Of Cal Ripken's abilities, the one that says "I told you so" is understated but undeniably one of his strongest.

It's the driving force behind The Streak and a Hall of Fame career.

Ripken is not one to publicly respond to critics, but that's not to say he's not sensitive to what's said and written.

When *The New York Times* recently tried to undress him—portraying him as something decidedly less than a consummate team player—Ripken used a national broadcast on ABC to issue his rebuttal.

Such a public response is rare. Ripken usually reacts to heat with cool professionalism and determination. When the Baltimore Orioles fired Ripken's father as coach and released his brother, Billy, he hid his anger and spoke of the business side of the sport.

Throughout it all, The Streak continued, as did the home runs, the All-Star games, and his influence in the clubhouse.

When mounting games and innings seemed to take a toll and there were grum-

blings in 1990 that he should rest, and that it was selfish of him to try to preserve The Streak, Ripken's verbal response was that he played to help the team. On the field, he answered with his second Most Valuable Player Award, in 1991.

Now, more than two years removed from the night he captivated the American sporting public by breaking Lou Gehrig's consecutive-games record, Ripken faced the greatest threat to The Streak—and perhaps his career—this September.

His back was hurting and had been for more than seven weeks. He received daily therapy. Almost every day, he heard whispers that he should sit.

But he played.

"It would be different if I had the time and sitting down for a month would have helped me," Ripken said. "But, I didn't have the time, and I didn't think one day would help me. I

needed at-bats to get ready for the postseason. I needed to get my swing down.

"I'm not playing for The Streak," Ripken said, quickly adding, "but I'm proud of it."

Ripken plays every day because he's Johnson's best option and because of the sensitive nature of his historic record.

With no track record proving rest will help, who's to say Ripken isn't correct?

What if The Streak ended and Ripken was right—that one day didn't help? Why tamper with Ripken's psyche? Why test him on this?

Ripken insists he's not bigger than his team and no player is bigger than the game, but teammate Brady Anderson says, "He's the most famous baseball player in the world. He's a living baseball legend."

Baseball's foundation is its history, and The Streak is about history.

Still, none of that stops the whispers that he should've rested.

Those whispers, however, can only set up Ripken's flair for the dramatic.

For a player whose foundation is consistency, Ripken has an uncanny ability to produce in the spotlight. The homers on the nights he tied and broke Gehrig's record only boldfaced and underlined his "I told you so" response to those who suggested he should have sat.

This postseason presents a similar opportunity.

A strong October ends the whispers. It's Ripken's best defense.

Five hits in the first two games in Seattle have been a solid opening statement.

"When people say I can't do something," Ripken says, "it makes me try that much harder." ■

*While the baseball world was focusing on Mark McGwire and Sammy Sosa, the summer of 1998 provided another magical moment in Baltimore for Cal Ripken Jr. and Orioles fans. On August 21, 1998, Ripken singled to pass Brooks Robinson for the most hits in Orioles history. This piece originally appeared on August 22, 1998.*

# Ripken Is Tops on Orioles' Hit Parade

The batter grounded an 0–1 pitch into the hole between first and second and the cheers began. The cheers gave way to a roar as seats folded up and fans stood, celebrating what the scoreboard told them, in case they didn't know.

"Cal Ripken has just surpassed Brooks Robinson as the Orioles' all-time hit leader," the scoreboard read.

And the fans kept roaring.

Roaring for the man who had just taken the final piece of the torch from Robinson as the Orioles' all-time icon.

Roaring as they have for him throughout his career, which began back in 1981.

Ripken, who had just collected hit No. 2,849, stood at first, shyly acknowledging the cheers.

He chuckled at the way he made Orioles history yet again.

"I was looking for a curveball and I hit a fastball away," he told Indians rookie first baseman Richie Sexson amid the cheers. Sexson put his head down, laughing softly.

Ripken heard the 48,374 fans and he was no longer just on first base. He was everywhere. Streak Week. The World Series. All of it kept coming back, rushing into Ripken's head.

"You think about your whole career in a way," he said. "Those things flash through your mind. You wonder how lucky you are. It makes me feel good just knowing my personal feelings about the Orioles and how they're my team and always have been my team."

Indians pitcher Jaret Wright rolled the ball over to the Orioles' dugout, where manager Ray Miller stopped clapping long enough to pick it up.

Ripken took his helmet off and waved to the crowd, his soulful blue eyes showing that he was humbled by the attention. This wasn't Streak Night, in which the celebration for Ripken's consecutive-games record seemed to last forever, but it was a moment.

"I've had many moments where the fans of Baltimore have embraced me," Ripken said. "When there's a moment, it ties all the other moments together. The excitement builds again and it links all those things together."

"I've had many moments where the fans of Baltimore have embraced me. When there's a moment, it ties all the other moments together. The excitement builds again and it links all those things together."
—Cal Ripken Jr.

It was one more moment in the career of the Oriole who earns the most cheers when he comes up.

"Congratulations, Cal, on yet another milestone in your remarkable career," the scoreboard read.

Willie Greene, the newest of the Orioles, finally settled into the batter's box and public address announcer Dave McGowan called his name over the microphone.

The fans kept cheering, squeezing out their last bit of appreciation for Ripken until the first pitch was on its way to Greene. Squeezing out their last bit of appreciation for the Oriole who has put his stamp on the team more than anyone. Trying to make this moment last as long as possible.

"It's kind of corny, it's kind of weird," Ripken said with a thoughtful grin. "The reaction is so similar. The common link is each reception you get. It's all been very loud. It kind of gives you a real quick reminder of the others." ∎

*Cal Ripken Sr. died of lung cancer on March 25, 1999. In his baseball career, he spent 36 years with the Orioles organization, including 15 years as an Orioles coach and then manager. This story, published on March 31, 1999, looks at what Ripken Sr. meant to the Orioles organization and to his son, Cal Ripken Jr.*

Baltimore Orioles third-base coach Cal Ripken Sr., left, and Orioles batter Cal Ripken Jr. argue a called third strike with home plate umpire Jim Joyce during a game against the Chicago White Sox in Chicago, May 15, 1990. *AP Photo/Jonathan Kirn*

Tribute to an American Hero

# What Senior Meant to the Orioles

Sometimes when he's on base, Brady Anderson still hears the voice. The Orioles center fielder has heard it for years, well past the time Cal Ripken Sr. stopped coaching him.

In certain situations, it's as though his old coach is still just inches away, barking out orders in that gruff voice.

"All right, bases loaded, no outs," Ripken Sr. tells Anderson, his tone commanding attention. "Take a flat-footed lead and don't move."

These are the kind of stories you'll hear people tell about Ripken Sr., who died last Thursday of lung cancer at age 63. The memorial service was Tuesday, but his memory lives on. Lives on through the effect his no-nonsense coaching had in his 36 years with the Orioles.

"I still, whenever I had doubts about some things or wanted to reassure myself that I was doing the right thing, I would call him," said Orioles bullpen coach Elrod Hendricks, who spent most of his 38 years in the big leagues working with Ripken Sr.

The Orioles have been searching for a piece of their soul for the past few years. They are trying desperately to return to the winning formula that produced the success of the sixties and seventies. The formula was simple: get the fundamentals down, do things the same way at every level, and treat the smallest of details like the biggest.

It was called "The Oriole Way" and it can be found by remembering Ripken Sr.

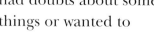

By listening to his stern voice. By looking into those hawk's eyes, which could immobilize you even as they comforted you.

"He could be harsh, but he sort of had a gleam in his eye," Anderson said.

He was a tough old SOB who believed in working hard. The rewards would come if you worked hard enough. And if they didn't, stop your crying and work harder.

There are so many stories about Ripken Sr.'s toughness and determination.

Cal Ripken Jr.'s favorite has always been the one about how Dad took a blow to the head from a tractor crank, cleaned the gushing blood, bandaged himself up, and went back to work.

And please, when you talk about Cal Ripken Sr., don't call him Ripken Jr.'s father, especially not around Baltimore.

Rather, Ripken Jr. is Senior's son.

That's the way it was, the way it should be. Fame should not trump reality.

In many ways, Ripken Jr. represents the rewards his father never got in baseball, rewards he had earned. But Ripken Jr. wouldn't have gotten those rewards if it hadn't been for his father.

He was a loyal, hardworking man who mentored some of the greatest players in Orioles

## Did You Know?

In 1987 Cal Ripken Sr. became the first father in major league history to manage two sons simultaneously. Cal Ripken Jr. was the team's shortstop and Billy Ripken played second base. On September 15, 1990, Cal Jr. and Billy became the first brothers to homer in the same game since Graig Nettles (Yankees) and Jim Nettles (Tigers) accomplished the feat on September 14, 1974.

history. All of that earned him less than a week in 1988. That's when he was fired by Edward Bennett Williams after the team followed a 67–95 season by starting 0–6. The man who had raised the best kids the Orioles ever had wasn't seen fit to attend graduation.

Bitter as he was, Ripken Sr. returned as a third-base coach the next season, only to be let go three years later.

It was a painful experience. Painful enough for Ripken Sr. to momentarily let down the gate his private nature erected and admit to certain people that he felt betrayed.

Tributes to an American Hero

Cal Ripken Sr. waves his cap to the fans.

"I don't think that that ever left," Hendricks said.

And so for all of his accomplishments—all the gratitude and loyalty of an endless number of successful big leaguers—it was his son who filled the void left by his own career.

His son proved what he already knew about the nature of baseball. The right way can work. Busting your butt pays off.

It had to feel good to see his son become the most dependable player in the history of the game. To know his boy was made of iron, mostly because he himself was made of steel.

"Asked in the old days about his greatest experience or some similar question, Dad always said it hadn't happened yet," Ripken wrote in his autobiography, published two years after he broke Lou Gehrig's consecutive-games streak. "After September 6, 1995, he told the crowd in a parade at Aberdeen that now it probably had."

There's a story Ripken Jr. uses in his book to tell his dad how he feels about him. The two men rarely expressed their feelings for each other vocally, but they found other ways.

So when Senior was inducted into the Orioles Hall of Fame in 1996, his son had a difficult time talking about him at the banquet. Instead he told a story about his children, Rachel and Ryan, bickering in the backseat of his car one day.

"You're just trying to be like Daddy," Rachel told Ryan.

Ripken Jr. thought for a moment.

"What's wrong with trying to be like Dad?" he said.

At the banquet, he added, "That's what I've always tried to do."

So have the players, coaches, and managers who can still hear Senior's gruff voice and see the gleam in his eye. ∎

*O*n Sunday,
June 13,
1999, Cal Ripken
Jr. went 6–for–6 in
the Orioles' 22–1
victory over the
Braves at Turner
Field in Atlanta.
The 38-year-old
Ripken, who had
spent time on the
disabled list for the
first time in his
career earlier in the
season, upped his
average to .328. He
went on to finish the
season with a .340
batting average.
This article was
published on June
15, 1999.

# A Rip-Roaring Game for Cal

Cal Ripken Jr. woke up Monday morning and, for a moment, entered that strange world trapped between dreams and reality.

"You wake up, your eyes open, and you wonder if it really happened or if you dreamed it," Ripken said. "It's nice to know it really happened."

Oh, it happened all right. The fans in Atlanta's Turner Field saw it happen. So did the national television audience watching on ESPN. They saw Ripken do it all again.

Six at-bats. Six hits. Two home runs. Six RBIs. Five runs scored.

Forget the stats. The numbers from the Orioles' 22–1 thrashing of the Braves can be calculated forever.

But if you're an Orioles fan—a baseball fan—just think back to yet another night Ripken gave you to savor. He was supposed to be done with these nights. Man, it seemed that way, didn't it?

Think back to April 19, the day before Ripken went on the disabled list. His voice was barely audible as he whispered "thank you" to someone who wished him good luck on getting his back checked.

He couldn't get past the back pain. Couldn't get past the pain of losing his father, who died in late March. People meant well, telling him all those great stories about Cal Ripken Sr., but it was all too much. So was the back pain.

On April 20, Ripken went on the disabled list for the first time in his career. Many people took this as a signal of the end of his career. And sure, it had to be considered. The question of retirement loomed, no doubt.

*"He's absolutely amazing.
People say he should sit down and retire
and all he does
is prove everybody wrong."
—Will Clark after Ripken
had a big game in Atlanta in 1999*

It all made sense. He was too old. Too injured. Too defeated. It was time to call it quits. It would be too much for anyone.

But that's just it.

How can you try to apply the rules for "anyone" to the man who made a career out of showing he wasn't like anyone else?

Back in spring training, before the injury, before his dad's death, Ripken admitted this year would be a challenge.

Admitted he would have to prove he deserved to stay in the game just like a rookie has to prove he belongs. He answered all the questions over and over until the question about the possible end of his career came up.

That's when he looked you dead in the eye and took on the question like he has all of his toughest challenges: head-on.

"I'm not afraid of it," he said.

So the challenges became a little tougher and the Iron Man became a little tougher. No more streak. No more "invulnerable" body. But there still are nights like Sunday.

Nights when the later it gets, the more you want to see him at the plate. The goose bumps on your arms say it all.

The Atlanta fans roared for Ripken on Sunday. They were no longer representing the Braves. They were representing you and your

kid sitting at home trying to figure out why you felt like crying.

So, when Ripken got that fifth hit and stood on second base, they thanked him. Thanked him with a long, loud roar that felt like a giant hug.

"It was a super, super feeling to stand on second base and be recognized," Ripken said. "You could feel the support. The acknowledgment of the night, maybe the acknowledgment of a good career."

A career that no longer seems like it should end anytime soon.

"He's absolutely amazing," first baseman Will Clark said. "People say he should sit down and retire and all he does is prove everybody wrong."

The six hits put Ripken at .328 for the year. Before Monday's game, he had hit in 22 of 26 games since returning from the disabled list and batted .367 in that span.

The power is back. His spirit is back.

There are more great moments ahead for Ripken. That should be clear now. He'll get his 3,000 hits and 400 homers, but he still has more of these spontaneously magical nights in him, too.

The man who's made a career out of doing what most people think is impossible isn't ready to wake up from the dream.

That's the thing about Ripken. He puts you in that strange world between dreams and reality. It's a nice place to be. It's even nicer when you wake up and realize, yes, it really happened. ■

**Orioles 22, Braves 1**

| BAL | ab | r | h | bi | ATL | ab | r | h | bi |
|---|---|---|---|---|---|---|---|---|---|
| Anderson cf | 6 | 0 | 1 | 2 | Guillen ss | 3 | 0 | 0 | 0 |
| Bordick ss | 4 | 1 | 1 | 0 | McGlinchy p | 0 | 0 | 0 | 0 |
| Reboulet ss | 3 | 0 | 0 | 0 | Lockhart 3b | 1 | 0 | 0 | 0 |
| Surhoff lf | 3 | 2 | 2 | 1 | Boone 2b | 2 | 0 | 0 | 0 |
| Amaral lf | 3 | 1 | 2 | 0 | CJones 3b | 3 | 0 | 1 | 0 |
| Belle rf | 6 | 3 | 3 | 1 | Springer p | 0 | 0 | 0 | 0 |
| WClark 1b | 4 | 4 | 4 | 5 | Remlinger p | 0 | 0 | 0 | 0 |
| Conine 1b | 1 | 1 | 0 | 0 | Nixon ph | 1 | 0 | 0 | 0 |
| Ripken 3b | 6 | 5 | 6 | 6 | Seanez p | 0 | 0 | 0 | 0 |
| DeShields 2b | 5 | 2 | 2 | 1 | Jordan rf | 2 | 1 | 1 | 0 |
| CJohnson c | 3 | 2 | 1 | 3 | GWilliams rf | 2 | 0 | 1 | 0 |
| Figga c | 1 | 0 | 0 | 0 | JLopez c | 2 | 0 | 1 | 0 |
| Mussina p | 5 | 1 | 2 | 3 | EPerez c | 2 | 0 | 0 | 0 |
| Coppinger p | 1 | 0 | 1 | 0 | Klesko lf | 3 | 0 | 2 | 1 |
| | | | | | AJones cf | 4 | 0 | 0 | 0 |
| | | | | | Simon 1b | 4 | 0 | 0 | 0 |
| | | | | | Smoltz p | 0 | 0 | 0 | 0 |
| | | | | | Speier p | 1 | 0 | 0 | 0 |
| | | | | | Derosa ss | 2 | 0 | 0 | 0 |
| Total | 51 | 22 | 25 | 22 | Total | 32 | 1 | 6 | 1 |

| Baltimore | 502 423 402 - 22 |
|---|---|
| Atlanta | 000 100 000 - 1 |

LOB - Baltimore 8, Atlanta 7. 2B - Surhoff (16), Belle (4), WClark 3 (8), Ripken (12), Mussina (1), CJones (15), GWilliams (7), JLopez (14). HR - WClark (5), Ripken 2 (7), CJohnson (12). SF - Klesko.

| Baltimore | IP | H | R | ER | BB | SO |
|---|---|---|---|---|---|---|
| Mussina W, 8-3 | 7 | 5 | 1 | 1 | 1 | 4 |
| Coppinger | 2 | 1 | 0 | 0 | 1 | 1 |

| Atlanta | IP | H | R | ER | BB | SO |
|---|---|---|---|---|---|---|
| Smoltz L, 7-2 | 2 1/3 | 7 | 7 | 7 | 2 | 2 |
| Speier | 2 2/3 | 7 | 6 | 6 | 1 | 2 |
| McGlinchy | 1 | 3 | 3 | 3 | 0 | 0 |
| Springer | 1 | 3 | 4 | 4 | 3 | 2 |
| Remlinger | 1 | 1 | 0 | 0 | 0 | 0 |
| Seanez | 1 | 4 | 2 | 2 | 0 | 2 |

Umpires - Home, Cuzzi; First, Nauert; Second, Gorman; Third, Crawford.
T - 3:03. A - 45,738.

Cal Ripken Jr. set an Orioles record by getting six hits in a 22–1 win over Atlanta on June 13, 1999.

*On Thursday, September 2, 1999, Cal Ripken Jr. gave the Camden Yards fans yet another thrill when he blasted his 400th career home run off Tampa Bay Devil Rays pitcher Rolando Arrojo. This column was published on September 3, 1999.*

# How Many More Moments Can Ripken Give Us?

The roaring had subsided, but now it was building again.

The JumboTron showed Cal Ripken's face in the dugout and now the 39,172 fans at Camden Yards needed more.

They always need more with Ripken. How do you keep thanking a guy who gives you so many chills? Gives your goose bumps goose bumps? How do you thank a guy who makes you think in your toughest times, "Hey, I can do this?"

This is what Ripken did for those fans throughout the 17 years and 2,632 consecutive games from 1982 to 1998. This is what he has done again this year, even through the games he has missed.

At the beginning of the year he had to deal with the indecision of being 38 and knowing his career could be near its end. Then that became nothing, covered by an emotional and physical avalanche that included the death of his father and his first trip to the disabled list.

Then back came Ripken with a six-hit game, with the sweet stroke that resembled that 1983 MVP season. He closed in on 400 homers and 3,000 hits and everything was right again.

Until he went back on the disabled list.

One home run away from 400. Thirty-two hits away from 3,000.

The party was postponed.

It was rescheduled for Thursday night. He drilled that 400th home run in the third inning, in his second game back from the disabled list. And that's when it all happened again.

How many nights like this does he get? How many do we get? Ripken stepping out of the dugout, waving his arms, letting his eyes tell you how humbled he was by the moment.

"There's a certain honor to playing the game and I try to stay within that. But inside, you're going a million miles a second. I was running around the bases wanting to jump up and down like an eight-year-old kid."
—Cal Ripken Jr. describing how it felt to hit his 400th career home run

By the people.

"There's times when the game on the field meshes with the people who watch it," Ripken said. "So when those times come together, they're magical moments."

He gets it. Hardly anyone does anymore, but Ripken does. You can see the true joy in his eyes. The connection between fan and player that has driven people to the game.

He is the master of moments. Somehow, he always puts it all together. The right action, the right words, the right everything.

On nights like these, the world is his. But only because he's so willing to share it with everyone else.

So the cheers kept coming for Ripken as the JumboTron screen showed his face.

It's a little older than it was back in 1995, a little more worn by life. But there is always that boyish grin after it's all over. The one Ripken flashed throughout his press conference, which began with him pretending to turn off all of the tape recorders in front of him.

The grin was not there, though, when the JumboTron focused on him. There were too many other emotions going on then.

The cheers swept up into a louder roar to the point where they were no longer cheers. When they are like this, you just feel it. You feel the emotion, the impact between fan and player. And now Ripken came out again, goose bumps on goose bumps.

And this is when it happened.

He came out of the dugout and looked up to the stands even though he had no idea she was there. He saw her. He pointed to her. And that was enough.

"I happened to look at my mother and I happened to catch her," he said. "It's so like my mom to come and not tell me."

He thinks about the man who taught him the game, his father, "every time I come to the ballpark," he said.

But now he looked at his mother and the thoughts intensified.

"At that moment," Ripken said, "you think about your mom, your dad, everything."

After he finished his press conference, Ripken looked over and again found her.

"There's my mother," he said with a smile.

He hugged her. Tight. The photographers all snapped their pictures, that big old No. 8 stretched across Ripken's back as he hugged his mother again and again.

They didn't need to say anything. They just shared the moment. ■

*C*al Ripken Jr. singled off Minnesota Twins reliever Hector Carrasco on Saturday, April 15, 2000, in Minneapolis, and became the 24th player in major league history to reach the 3,000-hit milestone. This story was published on April 17, 2000.

# Murray Welcomes Ripken to a Special Club

He lined the pitch into center field, rounded first, and shook hands with his first-base coach.

He had done it countless times throughout his career, this most mundane of rituals for hitters.

It is done without thought or fanfare, a simple welcome from coach to player.

But this welcome was not mundane.

The coach was Eddie Murray. The player was Cal Ripken Jr.

And the welcome was not to first base, but to the 3,000-hit club.

"To meet Eddie at first base, that was a special moment," Ripken said. "Just the look in his eye and the significance of our careers, it was nice."

The significance of Ripken's career as an Oriole became even greater—if that's possible—on Saturday night at the Metrodome.

Needing three hits to reach 3,000, Ripken picked up one each in the fourth, fifth, and seventh innings to add another Hall of Fame achievement to a resume already full of them. And to unload the pressure of trying to become the 24th player to reach 3,000 and the seventh to do so while also having hit 400 home runs.

"There was a big relief after the hit last night," a relaxed Ripken said Sunday. "It was kind of funny running to first base. When they talk about the weight off your shoulders, that's not just a saying. When I was running to first, I felt like a 20-pound bag came off of me."

By ending his chase in Minnesota, Ripken gave one of baseball's most nontraditional parks another historic moment. The Metrodome, with its balloon ceiling and orange glow, has now hosted three 3,000-hit milestones, with Minnesota's Dave Winfield reaching the mark in 1993 and Murray getting his 3,000th hit with Cleveland in 1996.

The magnitude of 3,000 hits for Ripken is different than it is for most of his peers in the club. For him, it is a nice addition, but not a defining moment. That came in 1995, when he passed Lou Gehrig's consecutive-games record.

Ripken tips his hat on his first trip to the plate on Wednesday, April 19, 2000, at Camden Yards in Baltimore, a few days after becoming the 24th major league player to have 3,000 hits. *AP Photo/Gail Burton*

Ripken hit his 400th career home run last season. Now he joins the likes of Hank Aaron and Willie Mays and the guy who greeted him at first base, Murray, as one of seven players to hit 400 home runs and record 3,000 hits.

It all gets tied into those 2,632 straight games and 2,800 overall.

"I've never really played the game for the big, round numbers," Ripken said. "I figured they'd come from playing every day."

He had been struggling at the plate, hitting .176 entering the game. He admitted the last 100 hits "haven't come as easily" as the first 2,900.

So, he went out and picked up three hits in a game.

Of course.

Why not get three hits when everyone least expected it?

As he waited for reliever Hector Carrasco to come into the game in the seventh inning on Saturday, Ripken wasn't worried about what the pitcher would throw him.

He was more concerned with getting his world to return to normal speed. As he waited in the on-deck circle, Ripken realized what it felt like for basketball players frozen on the foul line by a timeout.

"I was trying to calm my insides," Ripken said. "To me, it seemed like everything was going 1,000 miles an hour inside."

The 18,745 fans in the Metrodome did their best to embrace another potential piece of baseball history, roaring as Ripken stepped to the plate. They had roared in the fourth and fifth innings when he singled, leaving him at 2,999.

The first pitch from Carrasco went over the catcher's head to score Albert Belle from third base. The fans gasped momentarily before resuming their roars. The next pitch came in. Ripken lined it to center field and that world, which had been zooming by, suddenly began to change speeds.

"I saw the ball go into center field and everything starts to slow down," Ripken said. "Everything was in slow motion."

He shook hands with Murray, who reached 3,000 in 1996, at the same base, the same place.

The fans gave him a four-minute ovation.

The Orioles, an almost completely different crew than the guys who pushed him out of the Camden Yards dugout on September 6, 1995, came out to congratulate him.

Albert Belle was the first to greet Ripken and he shook his hand. Utility infielder Jesus Garcia, who collected Ripken's baseball cards as a kid, hugged him.

They all came in from the bullpen. Ripken was surrounded, engulfed by a team full of players who have been watching him hitting on TV or in person for the past 18 years. He moved to the first row, where wife Kelly, son Ryan, and daughter Rachel waited. The kids are a little bigger now; bigger than when Ripken unveiled that T-shirt with all the hugs and kisses from Daddy during Streak Week in 1995.

He handed the ball to Kelly for safekeeping.

Ripken went back to first, lifting his helmet off his head and waving to the fans.

"Thank you," he mouthed.

After the game, Ripken signed autographs well into the night, helping commemorate the occasion for the fans who tried to fill in for his hometown crowd.

Finally, Ripken waved, causing one last small roar. The roar said thank you a few hours after Murray had said, "Welcome." ■

## Did You Know?

In 2000 Ripken became only the seventh player in major league history to reach the 3,000-hit, 400-home run plateau. He joined Hank Aaron, Willie Mays, Eddie Murray, Stan Musial, Dave Winfield, and Carl Yastrzemski.

*The fans at Camden Yards didn't get to see Cal Ripken Jr.'s 3,000th career hit in person, since it came on April 15, 2000, at the Metrodome in Minneapolis. But four days later, the hometown fans enjoyed hit No. 3,001—a game-winning home run against the Tampa Bay Devil Rays. This April 20, 2000, piece describes that special moment.*

# Cal's 3,001st Hit Is a Dandy

When he crossed the plate, Cal Ripken's teammates shook his helmet so hard the manager thought they might break his neck. His old friend Brady Anderson pushed him as far as he could, laughing like a mischievous younger brother as he did.

The fans who had come to Camden Yards kept roaring in appreciation of hit No. 3,001. They would remain standing long after the Orioles' 3–2 win over Tampa Bay, mesmerized by past and present.

On the JumboTron were some of the past highlights that motivated the fans to come Wednesday night. On the field was the reason they couldn't leave.

Ripken had done it again.

A big night. A big moment. A big home run. Ripken lined a 1–0 pitch from reliever Jim Mecir into the left-field seats in the bottom of the ninth to give the Orioles their third straight win and the 40,077 fans another memory.

He did it in a 2–2 game this time, doing to the Devil Rays what Kansas City had done to the Orioles last week.

"It's the most exciting play in sports," manager Mike Hargrove said of the game-winning home run. "[But] it's not very exciting for the hitter when he crosses home plate. The tradition nowadays is to see if you can break his neck or rip off his helmet."

His neck fine and his helmet safely stowed, Ripken had no problem with the celebration. Standing at his locker after another on-field interview and another autograph session with the fans, who didn't want to leave, Ripken smiled.

"I guess if you want to write a script, this would be the way to do it," Ripken said. "A tie

ballgame, a great reception in your first game back. It was a good ending."

Ripken homered on the night the warehouse banners unrolled to show Nos. 2,130 and 2,131, when he tied and broke Lou Gehrig's streak in 1995.

Ripken watched the banners unfurl from the warehouse again Wednesday, this time to commemorate his 3,000th career hit, which he had picked up in Minnesota.

He smiled when two of the "3,000" numbers remained unrolled. But then the familiar roar overtook him, as did his usual uneasiness. He acknowledged the fans' ovation, then waved to the JumboTron camera, hoping the game would resume.

"At a point, you want to say, 'Let's get this game on,'" Ripken said.

So they did. A couple of hours later, Ripken gave the fans a chance to celebrate all night without worry about interrupting anything.

They had a lot to celebrate. Another moment for Ripken. Another win for the Orioles.

After the home run, the fans were roaring as Ripken's teammates started running to greet him.

In the dugout, newcomer Mike Trombley turned to Jeff Conine and smiled.

"Is he big here?" Trombley asked.

Conine put his index finger and thumb a centimeter apart.

"A little bit." ■

A commemorative baseball and a miniature bat are among the Cal Ripken Jr. memorabilia that have been issued over the years.

*I*t was just after midnight on June 19, 2001, when word leaked out that Cal Ripken Jr. was going to retire at the end of the season. That afternoon, Ripken made it official, announcing that he was hanging up his cleats. That night he received one of the warmest receptions of his career on a bittersweet night at Camden Yards. This story was published on Wednesday, June 20, 2001.

# Time to Bow Out

The applause rises steadily as the fans watch the video scoreboard in center field.

It's the bottom of the first inning and people are still trickling in for Tuesday night's game against the Toronto Blue Jays.

Beer vendors scream and the smell of hot dogs floats in the muggy air, but this isn't a normal night at Camden Yards.

All eyes are on the video scoreboard, where a clip from Cal Ripken Jr.'s afternoon press conference is shown.

The applause builds as the video shows clips of Ripken's best moments as an Oriole. He catches the final out of the 1983 World Series. He gets his first MVP award. He breaks Lou Gehrig's consecutive-games streak.

The applause gets louder and louder until everyone in the crowd of 31,001 seems to be clapping.

The cheers spill into the first pitch, when Ripken's best friend, Brady Anderson, steps to the plate.

It's energizing. But it's nothing compared to the second inning.

## The Beginning of the End

Wearing a blue golf shirt and a pair of black slacks, Cal Ripken Jr. sat under an Orioles banner in the old B&O Warehouse that towers over right field at Camden Yards.

He looked out of place.

No No. 8 Baltimore Orioles uniform. No eye black. No baseball cap.

Ripken was in an office building, three hours before game time, in street clothes, with his wife by his side.

Meanwhile, his teammates were preparing for a game against division rival Toronto.

Ripken was here to say good-bye, three months early.

Late Monday night, it became public that Ripken had decided to retire at the end of the 2001 season—his 21st season in the big leagues, all with the Baltimore Orioles—to spend more time with his family and to concentrate on his passion for youth baseball.

On Tuesday afternoon, he made it official at a 45-minute news conference in front of more than 100 members of the media.

"The last couple of years, I've been noticing that I don't like being away from home," Ripken said. "I miss my kids' activities . . . I'm getting into other things."

Instead of making an opening statement, he shared his thoughts at that very moment. He said that walking into the

*"[I'll miss] the little things: you come to the ballpark and put the uniform on, the time you spend with teammates, the pure joy you get when competing on the field in front of fans."*
*—Cal Ripken Jr. upon announcing his retirement*

conference room with so many people waiting made him feel like he was getting married again.

Everyone laughed.

And the beginning of the end began.

"It's so much fun to be around him. I'm glad for his sake he can finally go home, relax, and think back on the most wonderful, miraculous career a player could ever have."
—*Rick Dempsey, Orioles broadcaster*

Ripken stretches at Camden Yards before a game.

## The Best Friend

Brady Anderson knows most of Cal Ripken's secrets.

He was the only Oriole who knew ahead of time that Ripken was going to take a day off on September 20, 1998—ending the majors' longest consecutive-games streak at 2,632.

On Tuesday, however, Anderson had to read in the morning paper that Ripken had decided to retire this September.

When he saw Ripken in the locker room on Tuesday, Anderson approached him.

"I said, 'What the [heck]?' And he said, 'I was going to tell you [Monday] but you were talking to somebody,'" Anderson said.

Before this week, Anderson said he would have said Ripken shouldn't retire despite his poor offensive numbers this season.

Now that Ripken has made the decision, Anderson said he isn't going to argue.

"It's a very personal decision. If he says it is time, it's time."

Anderson said he'll miss seeing Ripken on the field, but he has a different perspective than most.

"He's one of my closest friends, so it's not like he is dying or going anywhere."

## His Worst Season

There has been speculation for the past few years that Ripken would retire and prepare for his certain induction into the Baseball Hall of Fame.

After 18 seasons of relative good health, Ripken missed half of the past two seasons with injuries.

He thought this would be a season of redemption. He hadn't felt so good in an off-season in years.

He then broke a rib working out in the winter and tried to push his rehabilitation so he would be ready for Opening Day.

"In hindsight I wish I would have taken longer [to rehab] in spring training," Ripken said Tuesday.

Although he wasn't physically ready when the season started, he was in the Opening Day lineup anyway.

And the season that has progressed has been his worst to date.

Heading into Tuesday's game, he was batting .210—more than 60 points below his career average—and had only four home runs.

Furthermore, the Iron Man had become a part-time player.

That, he said, is not the reason he is retiring.

"That was the question I asked myself, that was the tormented part, and honestly I can say, 'No.' Would I be able to stick my chest out a little bit further? Would I be happier and less frustrated from a baseball perspective? Absolutely," Ripken said. "But ultimately it wouldn't change the feelings I have for the other projects and the challenges that are ahead of me."

## Did You Know?

From May 30, 1982, until April 20, 1999, when Ripken went on the disabled list for the first time in his career, major league players made 5,045 trips to the disabled list.

## Watching the Kids Grow

There are names like Robinson, Palmer, Murray, and Weaver, but Ripken may be the quintessential Oriole.

He grew up in Aberdeen, 30 minutes from Camden Yards.

His father was a longtime coach and instructor in the Orioles organization.

He was drafted by the Orioles and, remarkably, has spent his entire career with an oriole on his cap.

"If you were to set out and write a story about the ideal situation, the ideal career for a baseball player, I think my story would have to be considered," Ripken said. "I'm a hometown guy. My dad was with the Orioles. I can't tell you when the Orioles were [first] really, really important to me, because I can't remember that far back."

It's that upbringing, however, that may have helped him make the decision to retire. His dad was never around when he was growing up. He hasn't been around as much as he would like for his 11-year-old daughter and 7-year-old son.

He wants to change that.

His daughter, Rachel, told him she was sad he wouldn't be playing anymore, but she wanted him at home more often. His son, Ryan, wanted to know if the retirement meant he would no longer be a player on PlayStation's baseball game.

And his wife, Kelly, said it'll be a challenge and an adjustment, but one she looks forward to.

"Sounds like I'm not wanted at home," Ripken quipped.

## The Next in Line

Ripken said he didn't want to put any pressure on his young teammates, many of whom are nearly half his age. In fact, one player, 23-year-old shortstop Brian Roberts, who has played next to Ripken three times in the past week, said he had Ripken posters on his wall throughout his childhood.

But if Ripken had to pick someone who could carry the torch and be the next great Oriole, he would choose outfielder Chris Richard, 27, or second baseman Jerry Hairston, 25.

TICKETS: 30$
PROGRAM: 5$

Seeing Cal one last time: PRICELESS

"If you were to set out and write a story about the ideal situation, the ideal career for a baseball player, I think my story would have to be considered. I'm a hometown guy. My dad was with the Orioles. I can't tell you when the Orioles were [first] really, really important to me, because I can't remember that far back."

—Cal Ripken Jr.

"That's pretty cool, really cool," said a beaming Richard. "It's something that is probably one of the best compliments you can get. That's Cal Ripken, he probably knows more about the game than anyone."

Hairston was equally excited.

"I can't believe he said that. He is the most respected man in baseball," Hairston said. "It threw me back a little bit."

Hairston then questioned whether Ripken had ulterior motives.

"I think maybe he wants to be my agent," Hairston joked.

### The Roommate

Former Orioles catcher Rick Dempsey was a teammate of Ripken's in the early eighties. He also roomed with the youngster in spring training and on the road.

"The kid was like a brand new pup, and a Great Dane at that. He was always bouncing around that apartment, always wanting to fight and to wrestle," Dempsey said. "I didn't have the energy to put up with him and catch every day myself."

Dempsey, now a broadcaster for Comcast SportsNet, said he'll never forget his experiences with Ripken.

"It's so much fun to be around him. I'm glad for his sake he can finally go home, relax, and think back on the most wonderful, miraculous career a player could ever have," he said.

### A Fitting Ending Awaits

Ripken's career will likely end on September 30 in Yankee Stadium.

Fittingly, it will end in the same place that Lou Gehrig—the man whose Iron Man streak Ripken broke—played.

The same place where Gehrig gave his famous farewell speech.

It's also fitting that Ripken's Tuesday news conference came on what would have been Gehrig's 98th birthday.

But Ripken said he isn't thinking about the end.

At his news conference, he said he wants to concentrate on the next three months.

And experiencing what he loved about baseball.

"[I'll miss] the little things: you come to the ballpark and put the uniform on, the time you spend with teammates, the pure joy you get when competing on the field in front of fans."

## The First of the Good-Byes

With one out and a runner on first in the second inning on Tuesday, the roar returns.

This time it's deafening.

Ripken walks to the plate and the crowd at Camden Yards jumps to its feet.

Ripken tips his cap. He raises his bat to the third-base side. To the first-base side.

The roar continues.

This ovation is only one minute long. It pales in comparison to the one in September 1995.

But it's honest. It's true. It's from the heart.

It seems worthy of the day when Cal Ripken Jr. first said good-bye. ■

*This story, published on June 20, 2001, took the pulse of the fans at Camden Yards on the day Cal Ripken Jr. announced that he would retire at the end of the regular season.*

# O's Fans Know It's Time to Say Good-Bye

To some, he is a hero.

Others say he is the essence of baseball in Baltimore.

Whatever he is to Orioles fans, Cal Ripken will not soon be forgotten.

Tuesday night, after Ripken announced he will retire from baseball at the end of the 2001 season, fans at Camden Yards reflected on their favorite memories of Ripken and what makes him one of the most-loved players in the sport.

Bob and Andy Bealing, both of Hanover, Pennsylvania, are lifelong Ripken and Orioles fans.

Bob Bealing, 38, said one of his favorite Ripken moments came on September 6, 1995, when Ripken broke Lou Gehrig's record for consecutive games played.

## Did You Know?

The Orioles drafted three players before Ripken was chosen 48th overall in the 1978 draft. They were third baseman Bob Boyce, outfielder Larry Sheets, and right-handed pitcher Edwin Hook. Bob Horner went to the Atlanta Braves as the No. 1 overall pick in that draft. Some of the other players drafted ahead of Ripken included Hubie Brooks (No. 3 to the Mets), Rex Hudler (No. 18 to the Yankees), Buddy Biancalana (No. 25 to the Royals), and Chris Bando (No. 36 to the Indians).

Ripken answers questions at a June 19, 2001, press conference, during which he announced his retirement from baseball. His wife Kelly is pictured in the background.

"He is just a classy man. These kids need class. There are too many idiots out there. The men think he's a hero, the women think he's a hunk."

——*Baltimore resident Ed Monroe on Ripken*

"The emotion in his face when he walked up there and when he saw his dad, that was great," he said.

Andy Bealing, 35, said along with that memory, he also remembers Ripken's performance in the 1983 World Series against Philadelphia.

Bob Bealing said that, above all else, Ripken's sense of commitment to the Orioles and the community makes him a strong positive force in baseball.

"He gives 100 percent. He signs autographs," he said. "And he's one of the very few ball players that's a team player."

Heather Miller, 32, and Kim LaVigueur, 29, said they attend about six games a year and have become Orioles fans since moving to Baltimore eight years ago.

Miller, who is originally from Pittsburgh, said it was easy to become a Baltimore enthusiast. She moved to the area just before Ripken began steadily approaching Gehrig's record.

"It was a pretty exciting time," she said. "It brought a lot of positive attention to the city and that was nice for a change."

LaVigueur, who moved to Baltimore from Boston, said Ripken still evokes strong emotions from his fans.

"Even before he announced his retirement, he got such an incredible cheering and standing [ovation] from the crowd," LaVigueur said. "That still outshadows anyone else. He's just well respected in the game."

Miller said some athletes wander down the wrong paths and it's refreshing to see a professional athlete who takes his position as a role model very seriously.

"He's a good player and he's just a good solid person it seems," she said. "He's no Darryl Strawberry."

Ed Monroe, a lifelong Baltimore resident, said Ripken is the ultimate blue-collar player. He isn't flashy and doesn't always make the most stunning plays, but he's consistent.

"He is just a classy man," Monroe said. "These kids need class. There are too many idiots out there. The men think he's a hero, the women think he's a hunk."

Monroe said although fans will miss Ripken on the field, he understands Ripken's desire to spend more time with his family.

And Monroe will be watching when No. 8 plays his last game of professional baseball.

"I saw him start, I'll see him finish," he said.

Kelly Sharp attended Tuesday night's game with her six-year-old son Nick. They get to as many games as they can because Nick loves baseball, the Orioles, and especially Ripken.

"His father is a Cal fan, so I guess it just rubbed off on him," she said, smiling.

Nick tugged on his No. 8 T-shirt and pushed up his black Orioles hat, which was slightly too large.

"Cal is my favorite. He is nice and can play good," Nick said. "I wish he could play forever." ■

*Before Cal Ripken Jr. announced his retirement on June 19, 2001, he was struggling at the plate, hitting just .210. But the Ripken of old soon emerged, and he went on a hot streak at the plate during the second half of the season. One of the biggest highlights came on July 14, when he slammed two home runs in his final appearance at Atlanta's Turner Field. This story was published on July 15, 2001.*

# A Night to Remember in Atlanta

With camera bulbs flickering throughout Turner Field, Cal Ripken Jr. stepped forward and made contact with a Steve Reed breaking ball.

When the ball jumped off the bat, it was apparent it had happened again.

Ripken had hit his second homer of the night—both rocket line drives over the left-field wall—in his last appearance ever at Turner Field.

And that wasn't even the most surreal part of Saturday's 4–1 Baltimore win over the Braves.

That came one pitch later, when the crowd of 50,069 remained on its feet until Ripken came out of the visiting dugout and waved three times to the fans.

"Unbelievable," Ripken said. "[It was] almost to the point where you feel you're doing something wrong in the middle of the game.

## Did You Know?

In 1991 Ripken became just the second player in major league history to win a league MVP, Major League Player of the Year (*The Sporting News*, the *Associated Press*, and *Baseball Digest*), All-Star Game MVP, and a Gold Glove all in the same season. The only other player to have done so was Dodgers shortstop Maury Wills in 1962.

Ripken connects for a solo homer in the third inning for the American League at the 72nd All-Star Game at Safeco Field in Seattle on Tuesday, July 10, 2001. *AP Photo/Elaine Thompson*

"I felt appreciative and I felt thankful for the support and it felt great, but I didn't want to interrupt the game. The faster you can make a quick thank-you-very-much and get back in the dugout, I think is respectful to the game."

Only Ripken in his final season could get a curtain call from the opposing crowd.

What's utterly amazing is that he received two curtain calls on Saturday night, the first coming after his two-run homer in the sixth broke a 1–1 tie and essentially gave the Orioles the win.

"He's a stud. Anyone who gets a curtain call in an opposing team's stadium is doing something right," second baseman Jerry Hairston said.

The sixth-inning homer, which came off Atlanta starter John Burkett (6–7) was Ripken's first in a regular-season game since June 16.

On Tuesday, he hit a home run in the All-Star Game against Chan Ho Park that Burkett caught while standing in the National League bullpen.

Since announcing his retirement on June 19, Ripken has excelled. He went 0–3 in his first game and has compiled a 15-game hitting streak since.

"He's a good role model for everybody, not just kids, but everybody. We need more people like him in sports, because most of them act like kids. They don't know how to handle money and fame."

—*York, Pennsylvania, resident Ed Orth on Ripken*

He is 21 of 59 in that span, an average of .386, and has improved his season average from .207 to .249.

Oriole manager Mike Hargrove said he believes Ripken is more relaxed at the plate since announcing his retirement plans.

Ripken agrees.

"Absolutely. Since I did announce my intentions to retire at the end of the season, there's a weight lifted off my shoulders," he said.

Hargrove originally wasn't going to play Ripken on Saturday. Before each series, he tells Ripken when he'll start and Hargrove originally had Ripken scheduled to play on Thursday and Friday.

The manager decided after Thursday's game to mix it up and rest Ripken on Friday and have him start on Saturday instead. He never told Ripken of the change in plans.

"I really don't have an explanation for it except that my baseball instinct told me it was the right way to go," Hargrove said.

Counting Saturday's game and his July 1 finale in Comiskey Park, Ripken is now 5–for–7 with two homers, five runs scored, and three RBIs in the two games that have marked his last appearance in a specific stadium.

The two-homer game was Ripken's 19th in his 21 seasons in the majors.

"He's a living legend. Not too many people get to play in the big leagues, yet alone with someone like that," said Oriole outfielder Chris Richard. ■

## Did You Know?

Ripken finished his career as the Baltimore Orioles' all-time leader in games played, at-bats, runs, hits, doubles, home runs, total bases, RBIs, and extra-base hits.

*Columnist Mike Argento wrote this piece, which was published on June 20, 2001, and used the moment that Cal Ripken Jr. announced his retirement as an opportunity to reflect upon his career.*

# Ripken Made You Love this Game

The first time we saw him, he was a gangly beanpole of a kid with black hair curling out from under his cap, that ugly, tri-toned job emblazoned with the Oriole that looked terminally insane.

He was 20. His old man was a craggy old coach, a guy who looked like he had just killed your dog and couldn't wait to tell you about it.

He didn't seem like anything special.

You knew he could play the game. You didn't know that once he started playing every day, he'd never sit. May 30, 1982, he took the field and through pain and injury and slumps and losing streaks, he never sat down.

When his team won the World Series in 1983, you thought it'd be the first of a long streak. He was Most Valuable Player that year. Game 5, you remember, he made the last out, in Philly, snagging a soft line drive from Garry Maddox's bat to close out the Series.

You couldn't know then that it would be his only World Series.

He's not considered the best who's ever played the game. He has talent, sure. But he has more. He has drive and determination, a mental toughness that makes him seem invincible. He has that thing that separates the greats from the so-sos.

You could see it. You could feel it.

Day after day, he played.

And he played the right way. He played the Oriole way. He followed a long line. Brooks. Frank. Boog. Eddie. And now Cal. As the years passed, he became the third member of the orange-and-black trinity: Brooks, Frank, and Cal.

He played hurt. He played on a sprained ankle, an injury that makes mere mortals immobile.

He played, though.

He never griped.

He never complained.

There were years he wasn't the highest-paid player on the team, when he should have been. He didn't pout and threaten to peddle his services to the highest bidder.

He was living his dream. He was a hometown boy playing for his hometown team. He loved the Orioles, and sometimes it seemed he loved the team more than the team loved him.

He played the game. He got to play with his brother. He got to play with his dad as his manager. He was playing when the Orioles fired his dad.

He played through it all.

And he knew it was a game. He knew it was a privilege to put on that uniform and

Ripken smiles as he holds the Most Valuable Player trophy at the 72nd All-Star Game at Safeco Field in Seattle on Tuesday, July 10, 2001. Ripken had a solo homer in the game and the American League went on to win 4–1. *AP Photo/Frank Franklin*

He was a role model, and he took that seriously.

He was steady. His life revolved around his family and his team. He still drove his kids to school and mowed his own lawn. He's the kind of guy you want living next door.

He was a big kid playing a kid's game. He always said he got the biggest charge out of going to the ballpark every day and putting on the uniform, and when he said it, it didn't sound corny at all.

His biggest endorsement contract was for milk.

The game failed you. Players went on strike. The World Series was canceled. Players and owners competed to see who could be the greediest.

He was there to remind you of baseball's greatness. He was there to save baseball.

You were there the night he broke Lou Gehrig's record on September 6, 1995. Your eyes filled with tears as he took that victory lap around the ballpark and hugged his wife and kids. It was one of those moments that made you believe in baseball again.

You knew this day was coming.

Ever since September 20, 1998, when, half an hour before the Orioles' final home game of the year, against the hated Yankees, he decided to sit one out.

He sat.

play his hardest for the fans. He knew he owed the fans his livelihood. He'd stay after games to sign autographs. He'd sign until the line ran out or they locked up the ballpark. He never charged $10 for an autograph.

He knew he was one of the luckiest people on the face of the earth. He knew he was living a charmed life.

He never gambled on games. He was never implicated in any scandals involving drugs, women, or spitting on fans. He was always soft-spoken and never bragged about his accomplishments. He wasn't comfortable being the center of attention, but he handled it with grace.

For the first time in 2,632 games, the first time since May 1982, he sat.

You knew then that the Iron Man was showing some rust and his days were numbered. He looked old. He didn't have as much hair, and what he had had turned gray.

You knew this day was coming, the day he would go before the microphones and announce his playing days were done.

You knew.

But it doesn't make it any easier.

And all you can think to say is this:

Thanks, Cal. ■

Cal Ripken Jr. hugs his daughter after a game.